Growing Up Rich

Growing Up Rich
In
South Georgia

Tom Gill

authorHOUSE®

AuthorHouse™ LLC
1663 Liberty Drive
Bloomington, IN 47403
www.authorhouse.com
Phone: 1-800-839-8640

Published by AuthorHouse   07/25/2013

ISBN: 978-1-4817-7655-4 (sc)
ISBN: 978-1-4817-7657-8 (hc)
ISBN: 978-1-4817-7656-1 (e)

Library of Congress Control Number: 2013912561

Contents

Prologue

Growing up as a child of a sharecropper family in South Georgia paints an image of hard times but my memories are just the opposite. We ate three good meals every day and slept in a comfortable bed at night. My parents loved me and taught me a code of conduct that I still strive to live by. I was taught; don't lie, cheat, say ugly words or talk bad about your neighbors. Go to Sunday school on Sunday and stay for church. Say yes sir and no sir to your elders and do not talk with food in your mouth. I was also taught to look people in the eye when talking to them. Daddy said that people with shifty eyes were not trustworthy. When I was assigned to the White House Communications Agency as a Staff Communications Officer during my military career, my upbringing became a source of strength that saw me though some demanding situations. I learned at a very early age that God loved me. After I became a Christian at the age of fifteen, Jesus made sure my very own angel was there to lift me out of numerous deep holes I dug for myself.

This book is memories of growing up in the mid forties and fifties. It includes my twenty-three years service in the U. S Army, with almost ten years assigned to the White House Communications Agency, in Washington, D.C.

Those were challenging times for America and I consider myself fortunate to have lived through the period.

Technology advances have improved our capability to do more things faster than ever before yet we seem to have less free time today than yesterday. We spend more time seeing our friends and neighbors at funeral homes than we do visiting at their homes. Yesterday, we elected Statesmen, today we elect politicians.

My military career gave me the opportunity to travel all over the world and see with my own eyes how other people live in other countries. I lived seventeen months in Korea, four months in the Philippines and three years in Germany where my baby daughter Elizabeth was born. One year was in Vietnam in the central highlands with the First Cavalry Division.

My ten year assignment with the White House Communications Agency gave me the opportunity to travel to cities in Europe, South America and Russia, during four administrations. I have witnessed the good and bad in people from all walks of life. No matter how hard we try to live the perfect life, it is impossible because we are all flawed with sin, some more so than others, but by the grace of God, there is redemption available for everyone.

My Christian faith has been my guiding light throughout my walk in life. There is no way I had the strength to overcome hardships and obstacles placed in my path without the grace of God. I am a scarred Christian with many blemishes just as we all are.

Although I have walked through the shadow of death and witnessed the horrors of war and destruction during my tour of duty in Vietnam, God was with me every second. I wish I was a stronger Christian but I'm not. He understands me better than I do so I don't worry about it.

God has poured out his love on me each and every day. One day I will dwell in the house of the Lord forever and forever.

Chapter 1

Growing up in South Georgia

The heat from the crackling fire burning in the fireplace felt nice and warm on my hands. I had carried armloads of firewood to the house and stacked it on the front porch so that we would have enough firewood to stay warm at night. Even in South Georgia, the temperature drops to the middle thirties in the winter time. Being responsible for firewood was one of my daily chores and I did it without prompting from mama, most of the time.

At bedtime, the routine was to hold one of mama's nice-looking homemade quilts in front of the fire until it was good and warm, then race to the bedroom and jump in bed and wrap up in a hot quilt. That was the routine at bedtime. The fireplace provided the only heat for our home. Daddy and mama were sharecropping a small farm off Trudy road located about five miles from my hometown of Blackshear, Georgia. I was nine years old.

Waking up on a cold day with none of the comfort features we all take for granted today are not missed if you've never had them. Rural Electric Corp was running electric power to farm houses all over America, but they had not made it to our home. Lamps filled with kerosene were used as the only source for lights indoors. I remember hearing mama holler out, "Thomas, turn down the wick on the lamp before you smoke up the chimney and burn down the house!"

Our toilet was an out-house in the back yard. It had two seats but I never figured out why. Even back then we just didn't go to the toilet in pairs. The phrase 'restroom' was not part of our vocabulary either. A discarded Sears and Roebuck catalog was a common addition and served a very useful purpose in its final days.

The house was constructed of weathered unpainted boards with a rusty tin roof. Even when new, the house was of basic design with no facilities for creature comforts. A large porch covered the front of the house. The front door was in the center and opened into a hallway running from the front door to the back door. The main living room was the first room on the left and had the fireplace. Two bedrooms were on the right side and a small room used for storage was next to the back porch. Another bedroom was next to the living room. There were probably less than a thousand square feet of living space.

Our drinking water came from a well in the yard. It was also the water supply for washing clothes and taking baths. The slang expression, "go draw some water," was used when more water was needed in the house. I don't know if the slang way of describing extracting water from the well was a common expression used in the south or just my family's way of talking.

I didn't have a girlfriend at the young age of nine but in the event a pretty little girl asked me if we had running water at our home I was prepared to tell her yes, I was always running with the water from the well to the house.

Large mulberry trees were all over the yard. They made excellent shade trees and also served to help keep the house cool in the summer months. When the mulberries fell to the ground, my feet stayed a dark purple on the bottoms from running around barefooted in the yard.

A slight breeze would blow a lot of mulberries into the well because there was no cover over the top. If there were county health inspectors, they didn't bother testing our water supply. The well water tasted good and nobody died that I knew of so it must have been safe.

The house had a wooden fence around the yard. It was old, unpainted and need of repair in spots but nine year olds don't spend a lot of time worrying about stuff like that. It stood about four feet tall. I made the foolish mistake of trying to jump over it one day. With a long leap in a single bound, I went airborne but without enough elevations. My feet stuck the top of the fence, and I went tumbling. I figured it would be easy to jump because I saw where Batman leaped over a fence like ours in a comic book I read. It just goes to show you can't believe everything you read.

The yard was covered in sparkling white sand. Grass and weeds were not welcome guests in our yard. Pulling weeds and grass out of the yard was another job assigned to me. When mama glimpsed a weed sprouting, she immediately summoned her best weed puller, me. "Thomas, get out here and pull these weeds up before they spread all over the yard." Mama was real busy every day but she found time to worry about the really important things in life like having a clean yard. She was probably afraid a neighbor may stop by and find our yard full of weeds. I think a clean sandy yard was a status symbol to be proud of like owning a Cadillac Escalade is today.

Our living room was small with a fireplace but it seemed big enough at the time because I was only about four feet tall. Everything looks bigger when you are a short little kid.

At night time in the winter, every family member would congregate in the living room where it was nice and warm. A very thoughtful little boy made sure there was firewood stacked on the front porch to be used in the fireplace to keep the fire burning. We entertained ourselves until bedtime by talking to each other. Sometimes daddy would pull out his juice-harp and play a tune while my sisters and mama sang. My ability to sing in tune, sounded worse than Barney Fife in the Andy Griffith Show. When I try singing in church, little kids turn around in their seats and stare at me.

Mama made all her quilts in the living room. Every scrap of cloth was saved in a bag for future use when enough had been saved to make another quilt. The wooden quilt frame was hung from the ceiling so that mama could sit in a chair and sew the little pieces of cloth together. Instead of taking the frame and the partly finished quilt down at the end of the day, it was pulled up to the ceiling until she was ready to continue working her quilt making.

The sound of rain falling on a tin roof produces the most soothing sound effects for some good sleeping. Lying down in bed, wrapped up in a quilt listening to the rain drops fall on the roof, was a perfect setting for daydreaming.

Our house didn't have insulation so during a storm; the wind would make a howling sound as it whipped through the cracks. If everybody today lived in houses with tin roofs and no insulation, we would sleep better at night but unfortunately have a humongous electric bill at the end of the month.

Like a lot of farm houses built in the twenties and thirties, the kitchen was separated from the main dwelling and connected by a walkway. There were no fire departments protecting country homes so the kitchen was constructed detached for safety reasons in the event there was a grease fire.

Mama cooked on an old stove that used firewood for heat. The cooking service contained four removable lids were the fire could be stoked while cooking. A firebox ran underneath the cooking area where wood was inserted to provide the heat.

Cooking on a wood burning stove was a messy, time consuming way to cook a meal, but Mama did it day after day without complaint. Our meals were simple food but good and tasty. My favorite foods were fried chicken, corn on the cob and green beans. Whole kernel corn or creamed corn was also my favorite. I love corn. Still do.

We had plenty of homegrown vegetables to eat which included mustard, collards and turnips planted in a small garden spot in the side yard. In early spring, daddy planted corn, English peas, tomatoes, okra, string beans, radishes, butterbeans and squash.

Meat was in short supply unless daddy butchered a hog or slaughtered a cow. Rabbits and squirrels were shot and killed for food. My children and grandchildren squirm when they hear such talk but it was a common meat staple when I was growing up. Having to eat a lot of wild life was primarily caused from a lack of money, but just in case it was a subject for debate today, my main point would be that if it was good enough for George Washington and Daniel Boone to eat, then it was good enough for my family.

It's unheard of to go to the supermarket today and buy a hog or a cow. Instead, pleasing sounding and descriptive words like steaks, roasts, hamburger meat, pork shops and t-bones are used because they switch our thoughts away from where the meat originated to a very enjoyable sounding meat for dinner. What could be more tasteful than a thick sizzling steak being grilled on the backyard Bar-B-Q grill?

During the war, everybody was encouraged to have a small garden to help out the war effort. They were named Victory Gardens. Families in the country were used to having a vegetable garden but it was a new adventure for families living in town. A vacant lot would be divided into a number of small garden spots so that a number of families could plant and grow their own vegetables.

Going to Sunday school at Pine Grove Baptist church was always something special. Not because of church, but because other kids would be there and I could play games and do a lot of running with my friends.

During a hide and seek game one night at church, I ran into a guide wire anchored to a telephone pole, that caught me up around my neck. The impact slammed me into the ground hard enough to make me consider early retirement from the running game. Folks who know me real well have hinted I never was the same after the battle with the light pole wire.

Later, at the age of fifteen during a revival service at Pine Grove Baptist, God invited me to be a part of His family. We Christians call it being born again.

Pine Grove Baptist is a small country church located on Trudy Road in Pierce County. Attending Sunday school had a profound effect on me growing up. My young ears heard wonderful bible stories about the battle between David and the Goliath, Moses leading his people out of the wilderness and the miracle story about Jesus.

Revival services were being held all week at Pine Grove Baptist. I was fifteen years old when, during the service, God knocked on my door and I heard Him knocking. The revival preacher was talking in a soft voice, after the sermon, that Jesus was calling and inviting anyone and everyone who heard the call to stand up and walk down the aisle and acknowledge our salvation.

I said yes when God sent me my invitation. It's not all that complicated. Jesus Christ, who died on the cross so that everyone could be forgiven, asks from each of us to believe in our heart He is God, confess our sins and ask for forgiveness. That's all there is to it. It's not hard at all. Little children can do it. I am a Christian by faith and a Baptist by birth.

Like a lot of other families, I have relatives who are members of other denominations who are devout Christians. While attending Abilene Baptist church in Augusta, Georgia, I asked our pastor if he had any idea why there are so many religious denominations. Without blinking an eye, he said, "Tom, you know God is smarter than Satan. Can you imagine the turmoil Satan could stir up if there was only one denomination?"

Now Baptists require a little extra but it doesn't have anything to do with being a child of God. We must be baptized to be a Baptist. It's probably harder to be a Baptist than it is to be a Christian. Smoking, drinking, cussing, gossip and not attending church every Sunday is fuel for many Baptist preachers' sermons. Jesus called all sin equal but Baptist likes to list a few favorite sins to rile everyone up.

Baptism services were conducted in the Satilla River for Pine Grove Baptist church members. It didn't make any difference if it was winter or summer. The name of the revival preacher escapes me but it was Alfred "Sergeant" Strickland who baptized me in the Satilla River. Mr. Strickland was a well-known retired soldier, lay minister and carpenter in the community.

When you become a Christian, it's my belief God assigns each Christian our own special guardian angel. Climbing out of holes we dig for our self requires a helping hand and God has always been there. My special angel continues to work as hard as ever, lifting me up out of steep holes I've dug for myself.

Mama washed clothes by hand in a large galvanized washtub. The clothes were hand scrubbed on a washboard to get them clean. Soap was made on the farm out of potash, lye, this and that and a lot of other ingredients I can't recall. The soap didn't have that nice store-bought aroma but it got the job done. With none of the modern convenience found in today's kitchen, it was a full sunup to sundown job for womenfolk to keep food on the table.

Practically all of the food consumed was either home grown or produced by other farm families in the area. We were poor but so were most of our neighbors. Families helping other families were a way of life. A neighbor with a large field of butter beans swapped with their neighbor for some black-eyed peas or other vegetable they had grown. At harvest time, farmers would get together and work out coordinated days for cropping tobacco over the entire week so that family members could help each other on their selected day.

Although tractors and other mechanical farm equipment were gradually finding their way south, most farming in our community was done with a mule and plow. Small farms were referred to as one horse farms whereas larger farms were identified as a two-horse farm. Just because mules were used instead of horses didn't matter. Another five years would pass before daddy bought a one-row tractor.

The farm had an old log tobacco barn with a wood burning furnace for curing the green tobacco leaves. After a few years of use, the barn started leaning and continued to lean each year until it was too dangerous to use. All the nearby neighbors were asked to help out in building a new tobacco barn. A day which was convenient for everyone was selected and that day was called having a 'barn raising'.

The men began arriving around sunup with their hammers and saws ready to build a barn. It was an all day venture stopping only long enough to eat dinner prepared by mama and the other ladies who came over to help out. At the end of the day, daddy had a brand new, gas heated, tobacco barn. Nobody asked to be paid because the next time, it may be them that needed help with building a corn crib or a smoke house.

Tobacco was the primary money crop for farmers. It replaced cotton when the boll-weevil invaded the southern cotton fields and destroyed the entire crops. I learned later on that it was the Brantley

Company who had relocated to South Georgia from North Carolina, were responsible for teaching local farmers how to grow tobacco.

A few select farmers from the area traveled to North Carolina where tobacco was already an established commodity. Cigarette and cigar manufactures like R. J. Reynolds and Phillip Morris had their plants in North Carolina. These farmers came back home and taught other farmers how to grow tobacco and large fields of the crop were planted all over South Georgia.

Growing tobacco may have been a good money crop but it was also a very nasty way to make a living. The tar in tobacco plants is gummy and messy when the leaf is pulled from the stalk. Two are three leaves from each tobacco plant were cropped by hand every week until the stalk was empty. The first cropping at the beginning of each year was the hardest. Bending over and pulling off a couple of leaves full of sand and slinging them under your arm until you had a armful, was a gritty, sandy mess. Men and sometime young boys cropped the tobacco. Women worked at the barn to sting up the tobacco leaves on sticks for hanging in the barn.

We didn't own a tractor so the tobacco was hauled to the barn by mule pulling a tobacco sled. It took a lot of grit and pulling strength for the mule to pull a load of green ripe tobacco from the field to the barn.

Normally, at least two workers, called stringers, worked at the barn to prepare the tobacco so that it could be hung up in the barn for curing. Each stringer had two workers, called Hander's, who picked up the leaves in groups of three or four, and handed to the stringer.

Each stringer used a large spool of tobacco twine which was used to wrap each hand of tobacco on the stick by making a loop around the tobacco with the string and rotating back and forth on each side of the stick until it was full. Each stick of tobacco was hung in the barn on long poles called rafters and placed throughout the barn.

Our barn had four rows for hanging tobacco for curing. Four tobacco pickers could crop enough tobacco in a day to fill up a barn. At first, we used a wood burning furnace to dry the tobacco leaves. Large metal flues were used to distribute the heat evenly throughout the barn. A constant heat was required over a five day period to cure the tobacco leaves to a nice, golden color. Someone had to keep the fire burning twenty four hours a day each week and at a constant temperature so the leaves would produce a quality product for marketing. I was that person on a lot of days. Making sure the temperature stayed constant required a lot of stoking the furnace and adding and moving burning wood to keep the fire even.

Once the curing process was completed, the sticks of tobacco were removed from the barn and hauled to a shed for storage. I still have memories of being awakened early in the morning on the day we would be empting the barn.

Waking up at four o'clock in the morning to empty a tobacco barn is a hard way to start the day. Early morning hours had to be used so that the tobacco would still be soft and not dried out by the hot early morning sun.

After climbing out of bed and getting dressed, I would walk quickly across the dirt road in front of the house to the barn and crawled up close to the still warm furnace and curled up hoping it was a bad dream and daddy would pick another day to take the tobacco out of the barn. It didn't turn out that way.

Young boys with long legs, like me, climbed to the top of the barn and handed the dried sticks of tobacco to another person straddling the poles on the bottom row. I always volunteered to be at the top of the barn. Dried tobacco leaves are full of sand. When the sticks of tobacco were being removed, sand fell off and found its way inside your collar and filled your head with sand if you forgot your hat. I hated that scratchy feeling caused from sand down my collar. Boys love to climb so I was a natural to climb to the top.

The sticks of dried tobacco were stored until the complete crop was gathered from the fields. After all the tobacco had been cured, the process of removing the leaves from the sticks and stacking the tobacco on large sheets, called Croker sacks, was the next step Once enough sheets of tobacco was accumulated, they were loaded on a truck or wagon and transported to the warehouse in town.

Blackshear was a tobacco warehouse hub for South Georgia farmers. There were the Big Z warehouse, Farmers warehouse and the large brick Brantley Company warehouse where farmers brought their tobacco for auction. Large stacks of cured tobacco was tied up on sheets and hauled to the warehouses located in Blackshear or Waycross.

When the tobacco auctions began, it was a very festive time for farmers and city folk alike. Large sums of money were being paid to the farmers and merchant's downtown found that it was their busiest time of the year and most profitable. All the warehouses were full of workers lining up the tobacco in long rows and young boys hired to place identification and grading tags on each sheet.

The majority of the workers were boys from the city that I recognized from school. The thought crossed my mind as to how did those boys got hired instead of country boys who had participated in getting the tobacco ready to be sold? It was probably my first exposure to the axiom that it's not what you know but who you know that's important when it comes to getting the better jobs.

People in South Georgia love salted green boiled peanuts. It is a southern delicacy that a lot of people from up north have missed out on over the years. If I couldn't get hired with a good job in the warehouse, then why not become an entrepreneur and sell bags of boiled peanuts? That's what I did. Daddy planted a patch of peanuts every year for livestock feed so my source to make money was readily available. All I had to do was pull up the peanuts, pick them off the vines, and bring the peanuts to the house for boiling.

A large galvanized wash pot mama used to wash clothes in was ideal for peanut boiling. It takes a connoisseur of delicious boiled peanuts to know just how much salt, and how long to boil them in the salty brine, to produce the best flavor. I became an expert. I'm not about to give away my secrets on how this is accomplished. Colonel Sanders keeps his recipe of 12 hcrbs and spices a secret so I figure it is only fair that my recipe for boil peanuts remain a secret. Each bag was sold for ten cents. Walking around the warehouse with my box of bagged peanuts, I would holler out, "fresh boiled peanuts! Get em while they're hot—only a dime a bag." On a good day I could sell a hundred bags. Earning ten bucks would go a long way in buying school clothes and maybe a new pair of shoes.

Mama bought most of her groceries from Jackson's grocery store in Blackshear. Mrs. Jackson sold commodities to farm families on credit if they couldn't pay until the tobacco crop was sold each year. She used individual note pads to write down each purchase so that she and the farmer knew how much was owed. After daddy sold his tobacco, Mrs. Jackson was the first to be paid.

Supermarkets were still a thing of the future for South Georgia so there were a lot of small grocery stores, like Jackson's grocery, to buy food supplies. All the food products were stacked on shelves all the way to the ceiling, behind counters, and out of reach from shoppers. Customers would inter the store then hand a grocery list to a clerk for filling on a big shopping day. Ladders were used to reach the products stored on the top shelves.

Trips to town to purchase groceries at Jackson's grocery were infrequent and came about only when the need for basic staples like flour, sugar, salt and pepper ran out. It was always a time of great anticipation for me and my sister when mama returned home and emptied out the sacks of groceries on the kitchen table. She always tried to bring home a peppermint stick or some sort of hard candy for me and Carolyn.

Our new farmhouse had its own syrup making capability in the back yard. A large iron boiler was used for cooking the cane juice and a cane grinder to squeeze the juice out of the stalk was nearby. Horsepower to operate the cane grinder was provided by mule power. The mule was hitched to a pole used to turn the two large wheels that squeezed the juice out of the cane stalk.

A fire was started underneath the boiler to heat the cane juice and turn it into delicious syrup. The cooking process was slow but well worth the time required to make enough syrup to last until the next year.

Naturally, I loved cane syrup growing up because sometimes it was syrup and biscuit or nothing when it came to meal time. Today even though I love the taste and smell of homemade syrup, I seldom eat any. I guess because of the fact I had to eat so much as a child.

Cigarette packs today contain a large sign on each pack warning about the dangers of smoking. "CAUTION, SMOKING CIGARETTES CAN BE HARMFUL TO YOUR HEALTH. SMOKING KILLS; TOBACCO IS ADDICTIVE; SMOKING CAUSES HEART DISEASE; SMOKING CAUSES 85% OF ALL LUNG CANCER DEATHS; SMOKING HARMS YOUR BABY; QUITTING SMOKING NOW COULD SAVE YOUR LIFE; and TOBACCO SMOKE CAN HARM THOSE AROUND YOU.

That warning was not on packs of cigarettes when I was growing up. Instead, it was very common to read or hear a commercial from a medical doctor advertising for the cigarette company. "I would walk a mile for a Camel cigarette," the doctor proclaimed proudly in the commercial. "Winston tastes good like a cigarette should,' was another famous commercial. Movie Stars and Sports superstars proclaimed the virtues of the cool taste of a menthol smoke.

Daddy was the only person in my family that smoked. He would "role" his own cigarette with Prince Albert tobacco. The tobacco came in a bright red can with a picture of Prince Albert on the front. A readymade cigarette was a luxury daddy couldn't afford. Unfortunately, after joining the Army, I began smoking. The year I spent in Vietnam, cigarettes were provided free of charge. I would like to say the Army made me do it but that's not true. Thank God smoking has been a thing of the past for me for several years.

Just like the cowboys out west, guns were a necessity for farmers. The only gun in our house was a 410 shotgun which fired a single shot. Daddy taught me how to load a shell in the chamber, pull back and cock the hammer then aim down the barrel of the gun and squeeze off a shot while holding the butt of the shotgun firmly up against my shoulder. My marksmanship was good enough to shoot a rabbit on the run and helped me to become an expert marksman when I joined the Army.

When I was growing up, I make the awful mistake of believing my daddy was a weak, uneducated person who let others take advantage of him. Time after time, I can remember situations where those whom daddy did business with took advantage of his meek and humble ways to cheat and short change him in business transactions.

On one occasion, daddy was having car trouble with an old Nash Rambler he had bought the year before. The tie-rods where shot and when riding down the road, the front tires wobbled so badly the whole car shook enough to have made butter milk without a churn. Mama finally convinced daddy it was time to trade it in on some good transportation. Later that evening when daddy drove up in a Model-A Ford that refused to crank up when he shut off the engine, it became obvious a fast talking salesman had hooked daddy again.

Although I was just a boy, it wasn't hard for me to tell just by listening when he would be discussing buying a plow or other farm equipment or supplies that these sales people loved to do business with my daddy. I can recall the time when he purchased fertilizer and found out the bags where half full of plain yard dirt.

On another occasion, daddy had spent the month of February and most of March plowing the field with a single furrow plow pulled by his faithful mule. Plowing was something I could handle so daddy let me help him. We would start at the outer perimeter of the field and work toward the center. Normally, he planted mostly corn and a few peanuts for feed. His main money crop was tobacco. After planting the corn and peanut seeds, nothing came up. The feed store had sold daddy seed that was so old the seeds would not sprout.

Although I was just a young boy, I remember being a witness to these disturbing events and making a silent vow that when I grew up, I would never allow anyone to take advantage of me like that. It was the common denominator which drove me to be the best that I could be in whatever task I was involved in. I was as good as everyone and no better than anyone. Unfortunately, what I didn't realize at the time was my daddy was not a week and ignorant person. He was a meek, humble, and honest man who saw good in others but suffered in silence when being taken advantage of. His weakest links were actually his strongest parts.

Daddy was a man of few words but when he did have something to say, he had a sense of humor and loved telling little stories that I thought were silly at the time. Sort of like some of the stuff I write about. He could also play a juice harp and a few songs on a harmonica. In the winter time when there was nothing to do indoors but eat and sleep, my sisters and mama and daddy would sing songs with daddy playing the juice harp or harmonica. After a couple of try-outs, they never invited me back to sing along with them. I guess that's why little kids turn around in church when I try to sing and stare at me.

I wish daddy was alive today so that I could apologize to him. He died at the age of sixty-one from Leukemia. He was a good, uncomplicated man who trusted people. His demeanor which I took as weakness of character was actually God given strengths that we all could benefit from. It was my daddy who taught me to let my word be my bond. His book learning was limited to the ninth grade but his God given wisdom was priceless.

When I see daddy in heaven, it will be a sweet and joyful time to give my daddy a big hug and tell him how proud I am to be able to call him daddy.

We didn't have a refrigerator or a freezer, so meat and other perishables were preserved by smoking or salting the meat. We had a smokehouse in the backyard where the meat could be hung-up on pole rafters with a smoldering fire of oak wood burning to keep the meat from spoiling. Vegetables were preserved in jars for later use.

There was an Ice House in Waycross which sold large blocks of ice for use by folks that didn't have electricity in their homes. Instead of refrigerators, those homes had "ice boxes" for storing their perishable food. At least once a week, a large block of ice could be purchased when the ice truck driver arrived. The Iceman used ice tongs to grab the large block of ice and carry it to the homemade wooden ice box in the house.

When sweet potatoes were harvested, they were stacked up in piles and covered with pine straw then covered completely with dirt. This method kept the sweet potatoes nice and fresh and protected against freezing in wintertime. I had a lot of little jobs like scratching out some potatoes at mealtime that interfered with my playtime but I was still able to survive my childhood years and become an expert at playing.

I loved to play—still do. It takes a good imagination to be able to tackle the finer points of playing and I thought I was one of the best. It takes toys to play with the big boys and I didn't have any so I made my own. Every boy worth his salt loves to play cowboys and Indians. The game requires pistols, rifles, horses, bows and arrows and a pistol belt laced with bullets. With a pocket knife, discarded tire inter-tube, tobacco stick and twine along with some select branches from small trees growing in the woods, I made them all.

My favorite was my six shooter pistol. Now I have a very active imagination but even little kids have to have a reference point in making toys and playing games. My ideas came from comic books. My neighbor at the end of the lane from our farm house had stacks and stacks of comic books. He was a grown man but had a room full of every type of comic book published at the time. I guess he knew that one day the books would be worth a fortune because he never gave me a comic book but would let me read them at his house.

It took some time to whittle out my pistol but it turned into a masterpiece, at least to me. The revolving six shot cylinder was made from a discarded empty thread spool. The firing hammer was made from a small nail. The trigger guard was also made with a bigger nail bent around the trigger which was, guess what?—Another nail. Completing my entrée of toys was my pistol belt made out of a discarded tire inner-tube. Chicken feathers were used to make the guidance system for my arrows. It took lots of searching through the woods to find a branch straight enough to use for an arrow. I found out arrows will not shoot straight if the shaft is crooked.

Please don't giggle but my horse was made out of a tobacco stick. Tobacco twine worked perfectly for making the bridle and reins. My good friend Shannon and I raced our horses at full throttle galloping down the lane on our tobacco sticks. My legs were longer than his so my horse was the fastest. The reverse was true when we raced each other on our tri-cycles. I never could prove it but always suspected that Shannon's tri-cycle had a hidden afterburner built in because he always beat me racing to the branch between our homes. These memories slipped in somehow so let me regress in time to when these events occurred.

I was five or six years old when we lived by Earl and Sara Jane Walker. It was a small frame house mama and daddy rented from a local businessman named Lonnie Sweat. I never met Mr. Sweat but he had to be a very good person from all the nice things I remember mama and daddy saying about him. Instead of paying rent, daddy took care of chipping the pine tar from the trees in the woods that Mr. Sweat owned.

My sister Dorothy moved to Deland, Florida when she was eighteen. She was working as a switchboard operator when along came a sailor from Tennessee who knocked her off her feet. I have a slight memory of Dot bringing RJ Rye home to introduce him to mama and daddy. They were probably already married and were just giving the good news to mama and daddy for their blessings.

RJ was discharged from the Navy shortly after their marriage when they moved to Erin, Tennessee. I was eight years old when this was all happening so my brain wasn't fully developed and my memories of Dot are fleeting except for my first trip to Tennessee at the age of around thirteen.

It was the summer of 1950 when Dot and RJ came down from the mountains to spend a week at our farmhouse. When they started back up to Erin, it was decided that Carolyn and I could go home with them and stay a week and return back to South Georgia on the train.

RJ and Dot had driven their pickup truck to South Georgia so on the trip back to Tennessee, Carolyn and I rode in the back of the truck. A bench was placed in the bed of the truck up next to the cab and strapped down. This would be our seat to see country we could only dream about. The weather in July of 1948 was just about as hot as it gets today, but when you're a kid hot weather doesn't seem to bother you.

God gives kids special little valves called sweat glands, which open up and allows all the hot air inside to escape, all the running and playing is done on a hot summer day.

Our drive north was before the interstate system was built so we drove straight up the middle of Georgia on a two lane highway to Atlanta and on up to Chattanooga, then Nashville and on into Erin, Tennessee. RJ was a good driver, especially when passing another vehicle on a curve in single lane traffic. Carolyn and I were holding on for dear life.

Homes in Tennessee are built somewhat different than homes we lived in on the farm in South Georgia. Dot and RJ had a new home and it was the first house I'd ever seen with a basement. We don't build houses in the southern part of Georgia with basements.

Contractors who tried to build a house with a basement in South Georgia stood a good chance of striking water. RJ gave me my first lesson on how to be conservative with all material things. Their home was new and had a large basement with a wood burning furnace installed to circulate hot air throughout the house. I remember watching RJ chop up firewood in the yard to be used for fuel in the furnace. Nothing was wasted. Every sliver of wood chip was saved. When I asked him why he was saving the little small slivers of wood, he said those made good kindling to start the fire.

Vegetables grown in the hill country doesn't taste the same as vegetables grown in sandy soil. It doesn't matter to me where they are grown; I just love a good fresh tomato picked right off the vine.

The hills made bicycle riding an adventure. Climbing to the top of a steep hill next to Dot's house and then coasting down the down side was some fast riding. Going down was great but the going up part was rough even for a twelve year old.

Our one week visit was up so Carolyn and I were taken to Clarksville where we boarded a train for our return to Georgia. Carolyn was in charge or so she kept telling me. I remember making her feel like she was in charge because the box lunch Dot made for us was in her possession. I think boys need more food than girls when growing up and I was smart enough to know that the sandwiches were in the box Carolyn had control of.

Our train ride home also meant that when we arrived in Atlanta, we had to switch to another train. This is where our return home got interesting. Actually, we didn't have to switch trains. The train switched for us. It worked like this. We stayed in the same section as the railroad folks re-hooked our train car to another engine. It wasn't a very pleasant event for us because I remember Carolyn telling the conductor that we must get off and catch another train to Blackshear.

The conductor probably never heard of Blackshear and figured we were making the story up. Anyway, the conductor finally convinced Carolyn that he knew more about the railroad than she did and he would make sure we both made it to Blackshear.

My brother, Wayne, was born prematurely in 1944. His weight was less than three pounds. He was so small his baby bed was a dresser drawer. Mamma would heat irons in the fireplace and wrap them in towels and put the irons around him to keep him warm. At the age of two and a half, Wayne developed Spinal Meningitis and almost died.

He had brain surgery, which left him severely handicapped physically and mentally. Doctors told Mama he probably wouldn't live five years. Wayne was a fighter! His last ten years was in the Pierce County Nursing Home in Blackshear.

My brother was always an inspiration to me. He never complained about anything. He was always happy even though restricted to a wheel chair and hospital bed and dependent upon others to dress and feed him. Many a day I would drive over from Waycross to see him and feel so much better because of his steady and constant cheerfulness. Wayne died at age forty-two. It goes to show only God knows how long we will live.

The fourth grade was my favorite year of elementary school. It was in the fourth grade when I started drawing horses and other things that boys in the fourth grade draw. My grandchildren, all six of them, think their Papa can still draw a pretty good horse. It seems to me it was in the fourth grade when I started making sure my hair was combed. For some phenomenon, girls were beginning to look a little different. My first girlfriend was in the fourth grade. Her name will remain my little secret, but she had a brother named Billy Cochran. Billy is a successful businessman in Blackshear today. Many years after graduating from school, I ran into my fourth grade teacher one day in Blackshear. I stopped to speak and asked if she remembered my name. She looked up at me and said she couldn't recall my name but remembered I was the student who drew pictures of horses on the blackboard. Teachers sure can remember! That's probably why they make such good teachers.

Daddy worked at the shipyard in Brunswick, Georgia, during World War II. We didn't own a vehicle so daddy either walked to the highway to catch the bus that hauled employees to Brunswick or hitched a ride with a neighbor. The year was in the early forties and World War II was raging throughout Europe and Asia. Cargo vessels called Liberty Ships were being built at the shipyard and my daddy was doing his part for the war effort. He was too old to be drafted when war was declared by President Roosevelt.

During the war years, every American was asked to sacrifice for the war effort. Our nation's vast industrial capability switched overnight from producing goods and services for families to producing war material. Blackshear and Waycross along with cities throughout America established drop off points for material that could be converted for use by our military. The automobile companies converted from assembling cars and trucks to building tanks, ships, aircraft and every other type material required by our fighting forces. Families were encouraged to gather up and drop off any material that could be used for the war effort like old tires, inter-tubes and scrap metal.

War bonds were sold and rationing was used to limit the purchasing of critical items. Each family was issued coupons to be used for purchasing such things as gas, sugar, tires, and other commodities each month. Black pepper and coffee were also items that were rationed.

A military airport was constructed in Waycross and the base was used to train pilots how to fly fighter aircraft. The single engine P-40 was one such aircraft and the other was the P-51. It was a common sight to see the planes fly overhead on training missions just above the tree tops. Sometimes the pilot would spot me on the ground and wave and tip his wing. The closest I came to being a pilot was building a model airplane. After numerous hours gluing the balsa wood parts together, my very own P-40 was ready to launch. The instructions said that after assembly to hold the airplane firmly and then throw it into the air like a baseball and it would glide down and land. Something terrible happened during my launch and my P-40 took a nose dive and crashed. Both wings fell off and the fuselage broke into. I never tried building another airplane and figured being a pilot would be just as hard to learn.

My oldest brother Elvin was working at the Glen L. Martin aircraft factory in Baltimore, Md., when he was drafted into the Army. After completing basic training, he was shipped off to North Africa. He participated in the invasion of Italy against the Mussolini regime. Mama would always read his letters to me when she received one. All mail during the war was censored by the military and all entries which they felt could be useful information for the enemy, was redacted. The letters then were photographed, shrank to a smaller size and mailed to the addressee. I guess this technique was used to make space for more war material. I was too young to grasp the danger my brother and others were exposed to during the war but learned firsthand when my military career took me to Vietnam during the Vietnam War in 1966.

Unfortunately, the war was unkind to my brother. After he returned home, his emotional makeup was severely damaged and he spent most of his life in and out of the Veterans hospital in Augusta, Georgia.

There was one bright spot for my brother though, he met and married a pretty little girl from Blackshear and they had one son. Jeanne raised her son Mike without any financial help from my brother. He is a successful executive with a large company and lives in Florida with his wife Nancy. They have two grown children. I call Jean my adopted sister because she is a special friend and lady.

When I was at Shannon's house, his mother treated me just like I was her son. Their farm house had electric lights, indoor bathroom and running water. This made them rich in my five year old mind. Although our economic standing was quite different, his family treated me the same as if I was a family member. After World War II ended and the ship yard was closed, we moved to the farm off Trudie road where I learned at an early age that farm work was hard and the work load was spread out from sunup to sundown.

At the end of the lane from our home was Pine Grove Baptist church. My mother was a member but daddy retained his membership at Shiloh Primitive Baptist church in the county. Church members were known as Hard Shell Baptist which was the predominant denomination in the early years of the settlement of South Georgia. My uncle Robb Gill was one of the more well known preachers.

My memory drifts back to going to church where uncle Robb preached. Our transportation was a mule and wagon so we would leave home early in the morning and stay at church all day. Each family attending church brought their meal with them and everyone shared their food on a long, wooden table outdoors.

Preaching continued until the aroma of all that food being spread out on the table overtook the preacher's willpower to keep on preaching. Every type food that tastes good was spread out all over the long table. The ladies of the church saw to it that some of the best prepared and tasteful food in the world was ready to be consumed.

It was another fun time for kids. We didn't go inside the church so our time was spent seeing who could run the fastest. Kids love to run, especially boys. I was no exception. I've never read this in a book but I think the running comes from growing pains.

Our bodies are developing new growth daily and that new growth has to expand throughout our bodies. The running is what allows for evenly distribution. Kids that run aren't fat. Grown people don't run like kids and that's why weight distribution takes on a totally new dimension for older people. Which brings me to my main point; it's not food that causes people to get fat, it's the lack of running. Try running a couple five miles in the morning. When you wake up in the hospital, you may be sore but you'll feel better later on.

There were no glass windows installed in the church. Wooden shutters were used instead and they were opened up in the summer time so that those inside didn't die of heat stroke. Air conditioning was not available at the time but everyone had a hand fan provided by the local funeral home.

Uncle Robb had a loud booming voice so even though we kids didn't go indoors, we could hear the sermons. Uncle Robb preached until he gave out then another preacher would jump up and replace him in the pulpit. Sometimes they could use up to three or four preachers in one day. I found it hard to understand their sermons but assumed at the time that the message was intended for adults only so didn't spend any time worrying about it. Members of the Primitive Baptist faith are some of the best people God has placed on this earth.

Every Sunday, mama made sure that we all got dressed up and attended Sunday school and church services. It was a short walk up the lane to church and farmers from all over the community attended Pine Grove. I was fifteen before I became a Christian but a good foundation was implanted from a very young age. I learned as a child that, 'Jesus loves me this I know because the bible tells me so.' Over the years, my special angel was always nearby to pull me out of some deep holes I dug for myself. When this life is over and I walk through the gates of heaven and spot the angel that appears to be completely worn out, I'll know that was the one looking after me

Today the health food experts have concluded food preparation in the forties was bad news for our health. Hog lard which the health experts claim kills people, was used to fry meat and a batch of nice fresh eggs in the morning. Mama also used lard when she made homemade biscuits so light and fluffy they would melt in your mouth.

Even after all these years that have passed by, I have this vision of mama doing her magic in the kitchen making a fresh batch of biscuits. She used and old speckled pan that was probably brought over on the Mayflower to do her handiwork The pan had a hole in the bottom with a piece of cloth stuck in the hole to keep the flour from falling out. After patting out a little dough and adding a pinch of this and that, mama would roll the dough around in her hands and in a few seconds; presto! A nice, fluffy biscuit was ready for the oven. Most my school lunches consisted of a fluffy biscuit with syrup poured in a small hole punched in the biscuit.

There were no insulation in the house and the wooden floor was built with cracks left in the floor so that when sand was tracked in, it was easy to grab a boom and sweep the sand through the cracks. That was my conclusion anyway.

There were major drawbacks though and the one I remember vividly is the cold air coming up through the cracks in the winter time.

My feet were tough from going without shoes outdoors most of the time but cold air will penetrate the toughest of feet.

Whoever built the farmhouse didn't spend a lot of energy on creature comforts. If you walked up on the porch and knocked on the front door, the back door would rattle. The house was up off the ground and high enough that a person could crawl under the complete house. It was a great place for spiders, snakes and toad frogs to make a home. It was also a good place for a nine year old kid to hide.

I don't particularly like snakes that much so I spent most of my hiding from mama in trees. I figured at an early age that mama's don't climb trees so that would be better than hiding under the house. My running from mama came to a halt when I took off running one day and climbed up a nearby tree. She didn't climb up after me but mama got my full attention when she said, "you can't stay up there forever and guess who will be waiting on you when you come down?" Her switch was capable of doing bodily harm and mama knew how to use it. The whipping left little red spots all over my legs. I was a slow learner but caught on quickly that running from mama was not a smart thing to do.

My best friend Shannon and I spent a lot of time together building memories which would last a lifetime. We shared anything and everything we had. We had bonded at a very young age and could just about tell what the other was thinking. After we grew into men, I was the best man when Shannon and Rita were married in 1958. Shannon was my best man at my wedding when Marian and I were married in August of 1959.

My sister Carolyn and I walked up the lane from the house to catch the school bus on the main road to Blackshear. The road to our house was a single lane not wide enough for a bus. It was a good half mile walk to the bus stop. Carolyn was two years my senior so naturally she was a lot smarter than I was. It didn't matter how hard I tried, she would always be two years older than me.

School is like a lot of other things that happen in our lives. We remember some things but forget a lot of other stuff. One memory of the third grade is of the pretty little girl sitting in the desk ahead of me in class. She was as pretty as a bouquet of violets. I was pretend to pick her blue violets on the way to school and bring them to her, but never had enough nerve to accomplish the task. To my knowledge, she didn't even know my name.

There was one other event that I have a good memory of. We had this substitute teacher fill in for a few months. He taught typical third grade material but had two other subjects he loved to spend a lot of time talking about; ballpoint pens and cast iron cooking pots.

Ballpoint pens at the time was a new invention, or at least to students in the Deep South. According to the teacher, it was the greatest invention since sliced bread and he had a bundle available for sale. The other item was cast iron cooking pots. He spent hours telling the class how bad cooking in aluminum pots were for people and that we would probably all die from cancer if our parents didn't stop using them and switching to cast iron pots that he just happened to have in abundance. I told mama what he said and her response was, "that's a bunch of malarkey. Your granddaddy and his daddy ate out of aluminum pots and they're both still alive." I don't remember the subject of cooking with aluminum pots ever coming up in conversation again.

Going to school in the fourth grade brings back memories of my formative years and the beginning of taking notice of who I was and how did I measure up with my peers. Children raised in town experienced a different way of life than those of us reared in the country. The majority of country people did not have the same creature comforts that were available to those in town. We lived a less Spartan lifestyle but it was this way throughout the south.

Riding a bus to school was a new experience and it was my first time attending school with city kids. Children are intimated easily in their formative years and I was no exception. The quieter I could be and the least conspicuous, the better I liked it. My self-confidence was lacking in many areas and no way did I want to expose myself for the opportunity of ridicule by classmates.

Kids in school can be vicious and gruel to other kids when a weakness is spotted. I recall this classmate that was shy and quiet who always stood off by herself. Her dress was dirty most of the time and her hair was disheveled and looked dirty. She wasn't fortunate like me to have parents that saw to it that my clothes were clean even though they did have patches and my appearance was neat and clean. A handful of kids loved to make fun of her and call her names. Many times I saw tears running down her cheek in silence. I wish now that I would have had the courage to have spoken out in her defense but I didn't.

It was my first time being around classmates whose parents had money and they wore clothes to school that was new and the latest fashion. At lunchtime, the majority of students would eat lunch in the lunchroom. Those of us who brought a lunch would assemble in a common area and eat together. I didn't have any money in my pocket but I still liked candy bars just like the kids with money. I remember as if it was yesterday the school bus driver stopping at a gas station in town to gas up the bus before we proceeded on the route home. When the driver paid for the gas, he had the attendant bring him two candy bars. The thought crossed my mind that he bought two candy bars so he could share with me, but I was only daydreaming. Carolyn and I didn't have a nickel. We stuck together on the bus and although I didn't ask her, she would of liked one of those bars of candy as much as me.

My school teacher was a wonderful lady that took the time to make sure all her students were grasping what was being taught. I loved to draw pictures of cowboys and horses and tried to make points with all my teachers by exploiting my drawing skills. When no one was looking, I would fill up the black board with some of my artwork.

Books were opening up a new way of life for me. My world was confined to the things around me until I learned to read. Reading was a great way to escape and build dreams. The history books described exciting stories about America and the world we live in. My dreams were to one day be able to see other countries in the world, in person, and God answered my prayers.

When the subject was math, the material being taught may sink in on a good day and fly over my head on bad days. I was too shy to raise my hand and ask the teacher for help.

To this day I don't know how she could tell the material wasn't sinking in for me. When it was time for recess, she would stop at my desk and go over the subject again like it was the first time. Twenty some odd years later I ran into fourth grade teacher in Blackshear. When I left the Oak Plaza restaurant, she was setting in a car in the front of the restaurant. I walked over and spoke to her then asked if she remembered who I was. She said, "I don't remember your name but do remember you drawing pretty horses on the blackboard in the fourth grade." Only a caring school teacher could remember a student after so many years.

Segregation was the rule of the land in the forties so black people and white people were separated in all walks of life. There were no black children in schools that I attended from the first grade to graduation day in 1956. Black and White people ate in different parts of restaurants and even water fountains were segregated. It was unheard of for blacks and whites to use the same restroom. There was one movie theatre on Main Street in Blackshear.

Blacks had to go to the balcony to be seated and whites were seated in the main auditorium. At the time, it never crossed my mind that this just wasn't right and why was this being done. Even though I was raised in a segregated society, I never heard my parents tell me that blacks were inferior to white people. On the contrary, my parents taught me that I should treat all people the same as I would like to be treated.

At the time it didn't dawn on me but for all practical purposes, poor people were treated no better than blacks in the forties and fifties. Discrimination is wrong no matter what's its basis. God tells us that we should treat others like we would like to be treated. The world would be a much better place to live if that was practiced by all societies.

Segregation was ended in America under the Truman administration. After graduating from High School in 1956, I joined the Army and was thrust into an integrated military.

Thank God my parents had taught me to treat people the same as I wanted to be treated so my adjustment was easy. I had never been around black people but learned quickly that they were just like me and everyone else except for the color of their skin. Thankfully, the segregated past of America is over and will never raise its ugly head again.

The population of Pierce County in the forties was around 11,000 people with approximately 2000 living in Blackshear. It is a small town that had a lot of charm then and still dose.

The Pierce Trading company, which was owned by the Brantley company, was the predominate business in Pierce County. The company owned thousands of areas of farm and timberland, a fertilizer business, hardware and dry goods store and the Blackshear Bank. At one time, the company issued script to their employees and tenant farmers in lieu of money.

The Brantley family was well known and highly respected citizens.

I was fortunate to have known three members of the Brantley family from my high school days. Edgar Brantley and I were classmates and his brother George was two years ahead of us in school. George was a very talented basketball player and was a major force in winning numerous basketball games for the Blackshear Tigers. Their sister Mary Lynn was a year or two behind me in school and pretty as a button. Pretty as a button was how boys described pretty girls when I was in school.

Living in the country limited my chance for spending a lot of time in Blackshear. Hard times were starting to improve somewhat in our home and an occasional trip to town was a rewarding experience. Going to the downtown movie theatre and enjoying an exciting cowboy movie was the highlight of the month. Roy Rogers, Gene Autry, Tex Ritter and a slew of other cowboys provided all the excitement a growing country boy would want.

While mama and daddy shopped for food staples, Carolyn and I would be dropped off at the theatre. The same movie would be seen over and over again but that was no problem. I was fascinated with the film making technology so seeing the same movie over and loved the cartoons at the beginning of the movie. The majority of the cowboy movies were in black and white but all of the cartoons were in color. Mickey Mouse and Donald Duck will always have a soft spot in my heart. The Road Runner was a true speed demon and faster than a flash of lightning. I enjoy a good Road Runner cartoon today as much as I did sixty five years ago.

With two dimes, I could buy a ticket for the movie, a bag of popcorn and a coca cola. Movies were so exciting to watch with all the action that seemed real and live. Roy Rogers and his sidekick would gallop at full speed after bad hombres with pistols blazing away. Smoke from the gun barrel filled the air. A bullet would finds its target and another outlaw hit the dirt. There were no screams or blood flowing from the wounds. Outlaws lost every gun battle and a pretty girl appeared in each movie smiling brightly while Rogers played his guitar and began singing, "Tumbling, tumble weed." The pretty girl blushed and then they trotted off together riding their horses into the sunset.

Gene Autry and Roy Rogers competed with Buster Crab, Lash Larue, Red Ryder and a large group of other cowboy actors for our ten cent admission fee.

Every cowboy had their own specially designed outfit complete with their six shooters. Red Ryder wore his guns backwards when holstered. When in a shootout with another mean and ruthless outlaw, he used a quick as a flash crossover maneuver to draw both pistols at the same time.

Lash Larue was dressed in black from his boots to his black hat. Like other cowboys, he carried two six shooters strapped around his waist but his weapon of choice was a long black, bull whip. Outlaws would tremble when they heard the crack of his whip. With one quick crack, Lash could knock a pistol out of the hand of a cattle rustler or stage coach robber before they could fire a single shot.

There was no television sets so film clips of current news were shown at the beginning of the movies. There were no soap operas but exciting action adventures, called Serials, which continued week after week, were used to entice viewers back into the theatre. Marketing experts knew just how to hook viewers. To add suspense for the next week film clip, the serial would end when it appeared to be certain death for the main star. An announcer in the background with the voice of a funeral director, would proclaim, "How will the Lone Ranger avoid certain death? Who will come to his rescue or is this the final episode? Tune in next week to see what action the Lone Ranger and Tonto take to escape from certain death." The sales pitch was so tempting everyone could hardly wait until the next week to see the next episode, that is, if you had a spare dime in your pocket.

My oldest sister Thelma and her five children moved in with us when I was ten years old. The year was 1947. Her husband Owen, battled alcoholism for years and it finally brought on a complete nervous breakdown. He was committed to a sanitarium in middle Georgia and spent years there being rehabilitated. Thelma was left with no means of support and five small children depending on her for survival. Our home became her refuge. The move provided security for her and my five new brothers and sisters and became a blessing for all of us. The farmhouse was small but by some miracle, a place to sleep was found for everyone. Living conditions may have become congestive, but the good news was I now had five more brothers and sisters to play with.

Dick was the oldest at five years old. I was ten so I had to take him under my wing and teach him all the smart things ten year old boys have learned. His brother Phillip was four years old. Dick and I would let Phillip tag along so that he would have the benefit of learning all the neat things we could do. Lynn was three years old and her sister Mary was two. I left it up to Carolyn to take Lynn and Mary under her wing. Boys just don't play with girls, until they become older. The youngest was Billy at one year old. We left Billy with mama and Thelma until he got a few years under his belt. Thelma and the kids moving in with us turned out to be a great big blessing from God.

Although just how we slept is not clear, I know for a fact that there were a bunch of kids in each bed at nighttime. With that many living on the wages of a sharecropper, something had to be done and Thelma was the answer.

King Edward Cigar Company manufactured cigars in Waycross and Thelma hired on as a cigar maker. Actually, her job was to roll the cigar with its outside wrapper when it reached her work station. Thelma was smart, pretty and driven to see that her children were provided for. The salary she made produced the funds needed to purchase a lot of items none of us were use to having.

It takes a strong, God fearing woman to raise five young children, work a full time job and still spend quality time with all her children. Thelma was that woman.

We lived off Trudy Road for four years. Mama and daddy thought highly of the owners, Mr. and Mrs. Howard Flowers, but the farm was small and working as sharecroppers, income was meager.

There were no electricity and it looked like there were no plans soon to run power cables to the house. Sharecropping on a larger farm would produce more income and finding one with electric lights would make it a much better place to live. I wasn't told all this by mama and daddy because they just didn't consult me in those days on their business decisions. My young age undoubtedly had a lot to do with it. The time had arrived when it was time to move again.

Daddy drove the wagon up the lane until we hit Trudie Road, then drove about four miles to the underpass where highway Eighty-Four ran between Blackshear and Patterson. It took two trips with our one mule pulling the wagon to haul all our belongings to Bristol, Georgia. On the last load, Carolyn and I rode in the back of the wagon with the furniture. I remember cars pulling up close behind us and if there were any kids inside, they would make faces at me and Carolyn.

My thoughts flashed back to the little girl with disheveled hair being picked on in school. It is a painful memory that damaged my self-esteem but I've learned we all have to go through situations that do not bring back the best of memories. I've learned that God turns bruised spots we endure that made us feel weak into the strongest parts of our makeup.

The mule pulled hard without complaint during the trip to our new home. It took all afternoon to go from the Flowers farm to our new farmhouse in Bristol. Children tend to adapt to changes faster than adults. Carolyn and I were no exception. This would be just another adventure in our young lives. A new school with different classmates sounded exciting. Making the best of it was our only option.

Our new home was bigger and had electricity. There was a light bulb in the center of the ceiling in each room. A long string hung down to turn the light on and off. This may sound unreal but I had never switched on a light bulb before. We had electric lights at school but the teacher or someone else switched the lights on and off. It was like magic to see the bulb light up and glow brightly when the switch was pulled. A pull on the string created instant action. 'Click on, click off, click on, click off'. "Thomas, stop that right now and bring in some firewood." Mama hollered. I couldn't get away with anything because we all know mama's can hear everything their kids say and do from a mile away.

We didn't get sick at our house. At least, not sick enough for a doctor. From birth to age eighteen, I have no memory of ever going to a doctor. When someone was under the weather, so to speak, mama always had a cure. The cure was castor oil. Castor oil cured everything, or at least mama thought so. You could be a pretty sick kid but a dose of castor oil would make one well fast! Most of the time, it was better to act well than take another dose.

Medicine was made to taste bad. Good tasting medicine didn't work because you couldn't find any. There was one medicine the "snake oil" peddlers started selling that excited those who took a swig and made them feel real good almost instantly. The name of the medicine was

"Had-a-call". After taking two or three swings, like magic, people said they felt better. The fact that Had-a-call was made with about fifty percent alcohol probably had something to do with how they felt.

Chest congestion always called for a "mustard plaster". A concoction of stuff was mixed together, placed in a hot cloth and placed on your chest. It was left it on for about ten minutes or until you felt the skin blistering, which was a good sign to remove the plaster before serious harm was done to your body. Once the Mustard Plaster was removed, we had to jump in bed and cover up. Instant cure had arrived by wakeup time the next morning.

Today, we tell our kids don't forget to turn off the lights when leaving a room. Children do not pay light bills and probably think lights are free and come with the house. When I leave a room and forget to switch the lights off, after two or three steps, a little voice comes on ever so softly, whispering in my ear to, "Go back, you forgot to turn off the light."

I remember when one of my well thought out games went sour and mama came at me with her famous switch to whip me on the backs of my legs. For some reason, Mamas always have good switches. The real good switches came from small, slender limbs off plum trees. There was none of this child abuse stuff when I was growing up. Half of the parents would have been in jail if there was such a law. Children were taught to obey their parents, without exception.

When I was a little boy I could run fast and hide quickly. Mama was trying to whip me for some infraction I committed and running and hiding was my only way to avoid a whipping, or so my little brain told me. A nearby tree was spotted so up I climbed. I knew mamas didn't climb trees. Mama didn't climb up after me but taught me a good lesson that running from your mama is not a smart thing to do. "You can't stay up in that tree forever. When you come down, I'll be waiting," she said. "The whipping will be twice as bad because you ran from me". For kids out there reading this don't run from your mamas. Believe me; it's not worth the extra licks when you get the whipping.

Growing up on a small farm taught me some valuable lessons. A workday was long, work was hard and I remember thinking when I got grown I didn't want to do it. There had to be better jobs then standing on your head cropping tobacco or looking up and getting sand all in your face from tobacco sticks being removed from the top of the barn rafters. You itch all over after hand picking corn and throwing the ears in a wagon. Daddy had one mule and farming was basically all done manually, at least on the farm where we lived. A workday normally was from sun up to sundown.

Nobody at our house had a watch so the sun was a good way to tell time. You stopped work to go eat dinner when the sun was straight overhead. The time of day didn't seem that important in those days. You were up doing something when the sun was up and when the sun set, you ate supper, took a tub bath and then hit the sack.

We did have a battery-operated radio later on and were allowed to stay up a few nights to listen to the radio. Now, the radio was a big box and the battery was the size of a car battery. At night, you could pick up Cincinnati, Ohio. Electronics were amazing even back then. It seemed to me that every time we were listening to something important, the battery would go weaker and weaker, and then the radio went silent.

I remember one night listening to Joe Lewis box Billy Conn for the world heavyweight title. Lewis was the world champion and Conn was boxing to take his crown away and become the new champ. Billy Conn was taking the fight to Lewis in the early rounds according to the radio announcer. It was in the thirteenth round when Lewis delivered a series of fast hooks to Conn's face and the fight was over. Old Joe Lewis retained his heavyweight boxing crown.

There were approximately one hundred acres of cultivated land on the farm. About two acres of tobacco was the main money crop. Growing tobacco and farming in general was done a lot different than today. It was all done by hand. We used a tobacco stick to punch holes where the plant was dropped. Each plant was hand watered at the same time. Once the tobacco plant was dropped in the cylinder, by pulling on a lever opened up two jaws at the bottom, which then released enough water and the plant fell into the soil. Some old farmer probably made a fortune when he invented the manual tobacco planter.

Later, after the tobacco plants were around chest high, suckering and pulling worms off the stalk became a weekly requirement. At harvest time, the tobacco leaves were handpicked and the cropped leaves placed in a sled. Our mule provided the horsepower. Four pickers usually could crop a barn of tobacco in a day.

The hardest part of cropping tobacco was the first picking. They were called sand lugs located at the bottom of the stalk, in the sand most of the time. You had to almost stand on your head to reach the bottom leaves. The leaves were good and wet from the morning dew. Slinging wet tobacco leaves up under your arm and getting wet sand in your face was a frequent occurrence.

A sled of tobacco was dragged to the barn where the womenfolk did the stringing. After stringing the tobacco, it was hung up on rafters for drying or curing as it was called.

Field corn was grown and saved for livestock. Vegetables, pork, beef and chicken were raised for self-consumption. We could live rich without money because the majority of our food supply was home grown. Mama raised chickens so eggs were always plentiful. Talk about having fresh meat, you've never lived until a chicken is caught from the back yard for the daily meal. Describing what happened next to the chicken that was caught will not be covered because there may be animal rights advocates reading this.

Flour came in cloth bags. Mama saved and used the bags to make our clothes. The flour companies printed some pretty bags with all type designs and colors. The old Singer sewing machine was used with a foot pedal for power and was a valuable and necessary possession in those days. It was a common thing to see patches on our clothes. Mama took extra care to hide the patch as best she could. It never occurred to me that we were starting a trend, by wearing holy clothes. Kid's today love to buy clothes with the patched and worn out look. It wasn't quite as popular in the forties. She also made quilts. All scraps of cloth and worn out clothes were saved for future conversion into a beautiful quilt. Quilt frames were hung from the ceiling in the main room of the house where the fireplace was located. When mama was quilting, there was very little room for anyone else because the quilting frame filled up the whole room.

Bristol, Georgia had a Post Office, a four way stop sign, but no signal light. The good news was there was view, if any, traffic jams and no fear of being stopped by a policeman. Families in the community were fortunate to have Smith's grocery which stocked a variety of groceries used on a daily basis and some dry goods required by local farmers. Bristol also had one elementary school building.

I learned how to play basketball and completed the fifth grade when we lived in Bristol. Mrs. Cobb was my teacher and basketball coach. It was her mother who ran the school plus owned the school building. Two homemade wooden backboards with basketball goals were erected on the outdoor playground. Although I was small in size and structure, there were two identical twin boys on the team that were our star players.

Both were bigger than the rest of the team and seemed to know how to dribble and handle a basketball better than the rest of the players. Our coach practiced long hours teaching the basic fundamentals of the game and how to play together. It was a dirt court so everybody played without shoes. Later in the season, a game was scheduled with the Blackshear team. Their mascot was a tiger and they wore nice uniforms. We didn't have a mascot and wore our normal clothes to play the game.

Late one evening the players loaded up in Mrs. Cobb's car for the trip to Blackshear. We were on our way to play the city boys and teach them a thing or two on how to play basketball. On the drive to the game, Mrs. Cobb reminded all the players that the game would be played indoors on a wooden court. She was a good motivator because she said it may be somewhat different than playing on a dirt court, barefooted but we could all adapt. As it turned out, playing indoors didn't have that much impact on the team and we won the game.

Basketball became my first love in sports and I practiced every opportunity I had when farm chores were finished.

There were no school buses so I walked to school every day. It was a nice little walk but boys like to walk, skip, hop and run so it wasn't a big deal. When Christmas rolled around, Santa Claus dropped off a used bicycle for my Christmas present. That was the prettiest bike I had ever laid my eyes on. No more walking to school by myself. Carolyn was in the eighth grade so she attended school in Patterson and road the school bus.

After becoming an expert bicycle rider, I rode my bike all the way to Mershon which was about five miles down the highway. Peddling was easy because the road was paved from Bristol to Mershon. My cousins Kenneth and Travis Weathers lived in Mershon. Their mother was my Aunt Jewell and daddy's sister.

They owned a small farm and had one of the largest barns in the community. The farmhouse was on one side of the highway and the large barn was on the opposite side. Living near a paved highway was special as far as I was concerned. Kenneth and Travis had new bikes that were super charged like Shannon's because they always went faster than I could when we raced down the road. It didn't dawn on me that it was the rate of peddling and not the bike that determined the speed. I've always been a slow learner on things like that.

The Kress 5-10—and twenty-five cent store was a favorite place to go for kids. I remember Mama telling my sister and me to go get washed up if we wanted to go with her to the "five and dime" store in Waycross. Getting washed up didn't mean you were over the hill and about to be fired but to find a wash pan and washrag and get the dirt off. We called Kress the five and dime store. Some people just called it the dime store. Your neighbors always wanted you to bring them back something from the "dime" store. Driving all the way from Blackshear to Waycross was a special deal. Going to the five and ten cent store made it extra exciting. Little things take on special meaning when growing up.

Driving over the Satilla River Bridge was also an adventure. I remember asking a thousand questions about the bridge. What was it made of, who built it and how come the bridge didn't collapse when cars drove across. There was one section all smoked up so naturally that pricked my curiosity. I wanted to know what happened and was told that a gas truck had crashed and caught the bridge on fire. Well, the next question was how did they extinguish the fire? Mama said the fire was swept out and to stop asking questions. The swept out part just didn't compute in my little brain. I could just see a bunch of men with booms all over the bridge sweeping away. Words were tricky for me even back then. Wonder what happened to the burned out gas truck? I was afraid to ask.

It was usually the month before Christmas when a trip was planned to Waycross. I remember going once before and could still smell all that candy stored in big candy jars. The distinctive smell of the candy, mixed with fresh cooked nuts and popped popcorn, produced an aroma that only little kids can appreciate.

Once inside the Kress building were counters stacked high with about every kind of merchandise imaginable. The store was laid out so that the merchandise could be viewed on both sides while walking down the aisles. Clothes, hardware, cleaning material, candy, popcorn, and thousands of other small items were neatly stacked in the store.

A perfume counter was also available. Various smelling perfumes doesn't give off the nice aroma of candy jars filled to the brim. The Kress owners were smart retailers because each store had its own soda counter.

Young boys and girls with money could hop up on a counter stool; order a Coca-Cola, Hamburger and Fries for a quarter. Ice cream sodas and fresh cooked chocolate chips cookies were also available. The soda counter was about two hundred feet long with counter stools all along the front. Well, two hundred feet is stretching it but it did seem to be extra long. Things look a lot bigger and longer when for little kids. Hamburgers were cooked on a grill. The hamburger patty was flipped back and forth until well done and then placed into a warmed up hamburger bun.

Right before it was time to scoop up the patty, the cook dropped both sides of the bun on the grill and let it warm up. Add a little catsup and mustard and then get ready to bit into one scrumptious tasting hamburger. It's the same technique used today over at Strickland's Pharmacy located across the street from Memorial Stadium.

Sara Jane Walker was like my second mom. She always has a smile on her face. Shannon and I did a lot of playing outside and inside their home, and Mrs. Walker always made me feel like one of her own children. I learned real early to hide my bad side from adults.

The Walker house had the first indoor bathroom in our neighborhood. Every time I went to their house, Shannon would take me in and show me the bathroom. It was his way of making sure I stayed up to date on the latest bathroom fixtures. They also had the first TV. It was a console model with a screen about the size of a nineteen-inch unit. TV's in the early fifties could only be viewed in black and white. I remember one Saturday, Shannon and me were watching the University Of Kentucky Wildcats basketball team play.

Coach Adolph Rupp was famous for producing some of the best basketball teams in the fifties. One player named Cliff Hagen was a six-four forward who knew how to play basketball. I remember watching him that day move the player guarding him into the center pivot and then with a head fake, dribbled around him and lay in a backhanded basket. I'd never seen that maneuver done before.

Many of the corncob wars were held in Mr. Walker's barnyard. Corncob ammunition was plentiful, plus it was only a short distance from the barn to the nearby woods. You need more than two people to really have a good war, so our battles with the cobs normally included Mitchell Joyner. Mitchell and I are about the same age. He has an older brother named Johnny and sister named Marilyn. His younger brother Estes was two or three years younger so we didn't let him play with us. We had our reputation to maintain.

Doing dumb things that stand a good chance of causing serious physical injury is part of the price of growing up for boys. It hurts just a tad to admit to some of the things we did together. Mitch and I, along with Shannon, loved to play "on the edge" games. We played one game that involved throwing corncobs at each other. They were our own special crafted hand grenades.

A well-dried corncob thrown hard enough can cause some good size welts to appear on the body at the point of impact. It seems our specialty was to come up with old water soaked cobs and fire away at full velocity. The three of us survived the games without serious bodily injury and grew up to be grown men with no outward appearance of brain damage.

Shannon did like I did when he graduated from High School. He left town. Shannon started driving a Coca-Cola truck for the Coke people in Waycross. His health wasn't the best due to having bronchial asthma. Shortly thereafter, he was told by his doctor to find a good dry climate to live in. Shannon was now married with one son. I was the best man at his and Rita's wedding.

The year was 1958. I was home on leave after serving sixteen months in Korea. Shannon packed up his wife and son and loaded everything they owned in a U-Haul trailer, pulled behind their car, and headed for Arizona. Nearly fifteen years would pass before we saw each other again.

It was 1973. President Nixon was battling for his political life to put the Watergate scandal behind him. I had been assigned at the White House as a Communications Officer since June of 1968. President Nixon had launched a series of trips throughout the country to tell his version of the break-in of the Watergate complex and that he wasn't a crook. I was the Trip Officer for the stop in Phoenix.

I knew Shannon and Rita lived in Phoenix so I lobbied very hard to get the trip. My communications team was in town three days before the event, which allowed me a little time to get together with Shannon and Rita. They had a beautiful home with a golf course in their back yard. The three of us went out for dinner and picked up our conversations where we left off over fifteen years ago. You can only pull that off with a select few friends.

The trip was a political event, so the Republican Party paid for the cost of renting the sound system used for the speech at the Civic Center. The cost to rent the sound system for a one-hour event was twenty-five hundred dollars. Quite a lot of money in 1973, but you get what you pay for.

The event was being staged in the Civic Center were the Phoenix Suns played their basketball games.

The coliseum was filled at maximum capacity with people bussed from all over the surrounding are by the white house staff. Demonstrators were roped off from the site by secret service agents. They screamed and hollered and also used bull horns trying to disrupt Nixon's remarks. My experience told me that a full coliseum packed full of noisy people required a professional sound system. Besides, I liked my job and it wasn't my money. The senior White House Staff Advance thought I was crazy when I told him the cost. He said he would have to obtain permission from a higher authority. I remember waiting in the hotel room with him when he telephoned and talked to George Bush to get approval. Mr. Bush was the Director of the Republican National Committee at that time.

Shannon and Rita had moved to Phoenix, Arizona where Shannon worked with the Pepsi Cola Company. Through hard work like we were both taught growing up, Shannon was now regional Sales Manager. His skill at marketing soft drinks had been fine-tuned to the point that both Pepsi and Coke wanted his sales expertise. You have to be a good salesman when you think about the contents when buying a Coke or Pepsi. It's a twelve-ounce can filled with water. A little bit of sugar and a handful of other stuff Coca Cola will not divulge because it is super secret. We drink them by the millions.

Shannon ultimately switched back to Coca-Cola and became State Sales Manager of Texas. Not bad for a South Georgia farmer's son. Shannon died in 1987. I miss him greatly.

The Callahan's were another pioneer family with deep roots in South Georgia. They were hard working, solid citizens of the county, with the majority of them members of Pine Grove Baptist Church. William Callahan and I played basketball on the same team. William was a year behind me in high school. He was a very talented basketball player. His ability to make all the moves seem so easy and graceful was his trademark.

My relatives from my daddy's side reside near the home place of Uncle Rob and Aunt Ethel Gill. It is known today as Gill Hill. Uncle Rob was a well-known Primitive Baptist Preacher. He was well respected in the community and devoted to his wife and children. I have a slight memory of going to church where he preached. It was an all day service. Uncle Rob was good, but those services lasted all day and required relief help.

When Uncle Rob ran out of words, another preacher was standing by to step in. Us kids stayed outside and played but the church had open wooden shutters for windows so you could hear Uncle Rob as he preached the good book on his congregation. I think one of the requirements to attend all day church service was your Mama had to be a good cook. Those attending service brought food of every type and style. The food was served "on the ground" so to speak and everything tasted delicious. It had to be good food because most kids don't want to slow down long enough to eat. We didn't have any fat playmates that I can remember.

Running will burn the fat off before getting a chance to accumulate around the midsection. Unfortunately, after growing up, we tend to do more riding than running. Our bodies develop weird shapes but we keep on riding anyway. Aunt Ethel was a pretty woman. I remember her as always being neat with her hair done up in a roll. It was a very prominent hairstyle back then. She talked with a soft voice and loved to wear an apron.

Although she never raised her voice in my presence, I'm sure she knew how to raise her voice enough to get the attention of her children. Most of Uncle Rob and Aunt Ethel's offspring reside near where they were raised. There were fifteen children in the family.

Linwood and Robert are about my age, with Linwood maybe being two years older. Elbert Gill looked like my Daddy. He could have passed as Daddy's twin. Elbert even sounded like daddy when he talked. When I joined the Army and moved away for twenty-three years, all my relatives kept growing up and changing so that when I moved back to Waycross, they didn't look the same as when I left. I'm sure I haven't changed all that much.

Santa Claus always showed up at the farm. He arrived at our home and dropped off gifts for everyone but no matter how hard I tried to stay awake and catch him in action, I always seemed to be asleep during Santa's visit. When nine years old you try your best to figure out how a big fat fellow in a red suit with a long white beard could squeeze through the narrow passage in our fireplace chimney. Besides, Santa had to be one smart fellow to keep from messing up his red suit from the chimney smut and keep the bag of toys from getting dirty. How he could land a sleigh with a bunch of reindeer on a steep tin roof was also confusing but I just figured anyone smart enough to fly around all over the world delivering gifts for us kids who had been good, was one smart dude. I knew that Santa wouldn't stop by if I had been bad because Santa was watching me according to mama. It seldom snowed in South Georgia so I could never figure out why Santa didn't swap out his sleigh for a nice big red wagon while working in our neck of the woods.

Daddy selected the prettiest small pine tree he could find for our Christmas tree. I recall Mama, Thelma and Carolyn doing most of the decorating because they probably thought Christmas tree decorating was a girl job but it was fun to see the tree brighten up with all the stuff they crammed everywhere a bulb or bow could be hung. Christmas lights were not available so tinfoil and tinsel were used to brighten up the tree.

The Christmas story on the birth of baby Jesus was learned at an early age in Sunday school but Thelma or Mama usually retold the story at Christmas. We were all raised to remember that Christmas was the celebration of our Lords birthday and the true meaning of Christmas. Nine-year-old children tend to pay more attention to gifts and I was no exception. Although I was raised to know that Christmas was the celebration of the birth of Jesus, it was well into my teens before the true meaning sunk in and realized how blessed I was with the greatest gift in the world. Gosh, God loves us so much that he gave his only begotten Son so that whosoever believes in Him shall not perish but have everlasting life.

Christmas day at our home meant huge bags of fresh fruit were a standard treat. Mama made homemade fruitcake, baked chicken and dressing with all the trimmings. It was the one time of the year when bags of oranges, apples, grapefruit, tangerines, pecans and sometimes bags of walnuts where plentiful at our home. Mama always tried to outdo herself in loading up the dinner table with special Christmas dishes like fruit salad, pecan and cherry pies plus homemade banana pudding. Her baked chicken dressing was made with cornbread crumbled up and included all the other stuff needed to make it taste so good. Hog killing was performed in December, which meant plenty of fresh pork was on hand for Christmas dinner. Freezers and refrigerators had not been invented so fresh meat was smoked for preservation. Mama always had smoked hams and homemade sausage hanging in the smoke house.

Sharecropping for Mama and Daddy was coming to an end. Through hard work and saving every spare penny they could, 1951 would be the year they bought their first farm. The farm was located about two miles from Blackshear and had one hundred and thirty acres. Around thirty acres were in cultivation. The farm cost five thousand dollars. It was a special time in my parent's life, to finally own their farm, or at least own it in part with the mortgage company. Material things were getting better and better. There were around ten acres of uncultivated land in front of the farmhouse across the dirt road. It was full of scrub oaks and a few large pine trees. Daddy cleared the land with his hands. Every time he had some spare time he spent clearing the land. Tree roots were burned out. Daddy would hook up the mule and pull up the small scrub oaks.

I was during the next four years we would see an indoor bathroom, hot water, electric stove, refrigerator, gas heaters, tractor, television and in 1955, a brand new Ford car. Well, not exactly. It was what the automobile dealers call a demonstrator. You could buy a brand new car for about $1900.00.

Gas was twenty-three cents a gallon unless a gas war between gas stations was going on. A loaf of bread for the city folks was eighteen cents. Everybody called it light bread. Mama saved the eighteen cents and made all our bread. She was still turning out fluffy and soft homemade biscuits up until she died at age eighty-two. 1955 was also the year I met my future wife, Marian Hilton.

Chapter 2

High School and Basketball

Playing basketball for Coach Wallace "Country" Childs and the Blackshear Tigers was a lifelong dream. It beat farm work any day. The Pierce County Board Of Education had recently hired Coach Wallace Childs as basketball coach. The label "country" got pinned on him before coming to Blackshear. It's my best guess it was because of his speaking mannerisms. He had a refreshing way of expressing himself. Mr. Childs was a pilot in World War II. He flew the two-engine PBY-5, Catalina, which could land on water or land. This aircraft was used to find and sink German U-boats.

Prior to moving to Blackshear, Coach Childs established an exceptional reputation as one of the best coaches in the state. His basketball team won the state championship at least two years in a row when he coached at Irwin County, Georgia. I was in the eighth grade when he became the Head Coach at Blackshear. It was a special treat to go to the games and see our team win most of the time for a change.

The Blackshear Tigers and Patterson Eagles fought until the final buzzer sounded, sometimes with their fists. Every game was nip and tuck up to the final whistle. There were fights breaking out between players and from the fans. The Board of Education finally stepped in and cancelled all future games between the two schools. A few hotheads struck the match that caused the fire which exploded into violence, eliminating the possibility of watching and playing basketball between two exciting teams.

Ninth grade was my first year of high school and high school meant an opportunity to play basketball for the Tigers. Coach Childs believed his players should be in good physical shape so we did a lot of running, exercising and a heck of a lot of practicing. I thought that my body was in good physical shape from all the hard work required from living on a farm. Maybe the city boys needed the physical conditioning but not me.

Practice turned out to be as hard for me as it was for the city boys. Like many successful coaches, he would scream, holler, yell and make the team repeat the same drill until we got it right I had been yelled at a few times at home so it didn't bother me. When you're a ninth grader playing with the real old boys in the eleventh and twelfth grade, making the team as a freshman was tough.

Coach Childs played a very important role in my life. Everybody on the team was taught how to play as a team and what it took to be winners. Working together as a team can accomplish things beyond the capability of one individual. We were drilled in how to win but he took the time to teach us how to lose. I remember him saying that after each game, there is a winner and a loser and on those few occasions were our team came up on the short end of the score, he would remind everyone that we didn't lose, just ran out of time. His skills as a motivator were remarkable.

Winning is an important part of life. We sometimes lose sight of what is winning. Winning, in my opinion, is using your entire God given talents to accomplish a goal or task, to the best of your ability. It doesn't have anything to do with scores. Losers are folks who do things at less than their full capabilities. We are admonished by the Lord to use the talents we are blessed to have. Being a team player is important in about everything we do in life. We can accomplish more with the help of others. We didn't have any super plays or super players. Our ability to win ball games became quite impressive though. We probably thought we were a lot better than we really were. Winning has a way of doing that to ball players.

We managed to run a little faster and longer from Mr. Childs prodding. A typical practice day consisted of a lot of running and drilling on fundamentals. We were a pretty good fast breaking team. A fast break is when you get the ball under your opponent's goal and quickly move the ball to your end of the court before the other team can react. Coach Childs taught us how to make the outlet pass to a team member who was breaking for our goal at full speed. A basketball can be passed to a teammate who happens to be closer to the goal at the other end, quicker than trying to dribble to the other end. It wasn't rocket science stuff so we did it pretty good. His role model in basketball was Coach Adolph Rupp of the University of Kentucky. Our plays resembled plays the Kentucky Wildcats used.

Nothing fancy, just good sharp passes and a few pass and cut moves. We also did a lot of tipping exercises in practice. That's where you try and tip the ball back in the basket after a missed shot. Before you can tip it back in though, you have to figure out where the missed ball most likely will bounce.

Our two forwards and center were exceptional re-bounders. Donald and Steven Bowen both had a knack for being at the right place at the right time when it came to grabbing rebounds. They were cousins so both probably had the same type rebounding gene. Jackie Dixon and Ferrell Dixon played center. They had the same last name but were not related or at least didn't claim kin to my knowledge. Jackie had such sharp elbows; it only took one crack in the head from his elbow to learn to stay out of his way. Ferrell's arms were so long it appeared like all he had to do was hold up his arms and the ball would fall in his hands. Both centers knew how to position themselves for a good shot at the missed ball.

Benny James was deadly from his guard position when shooting his long shot. Benny would dribble across the half court line; take about one extra dribble and fire away. All you heard was a swishing sound as the ball went through the hoop. McCoy Carter and I played the other guard position. McCoy was one of the best at getting the ball to an open player. I played backup at guard, forward and sometimes center, my junior year. Coach Childs called me his sixth man and convinced me it was an important position—he told me Coach Adolph Rupp had a sixth man. That's good stuff for an eleventh grader. If coach Rupp had a sixth man, then it had to be a good position. It worked for me.

The Blackshear Tigers won the state class "A" championship for the year 1954-1955. The final score escapes me but we won! The championship game was played at the city auditorium in Macon, Georgia. At that time, it seemed like there were over 10,000 spectators in attendance in this huge building. Actually, the auditorium could only seat around 2,000 people but that was a bunch back then for high school basketball. It seemed half the population of Blackshear drove up for the game.

Every player on the basketball team was awarded a sport jacket. It was white with gold and black trim. On the sleeve was a basketball logo with the words "1954 - 1955 State Class "A" Champions". It made you feel a little special when the jacket was worn. Back then, if you had a girlfriend, you let her borrow the jacket and she wore it. That probably meant you were "going steady".

Little girls wearing large jackets are a sight to see. The tradition of girls wearing ball player's jackets continues today. All the players also received a little gold basketball that could fit on a chain that said State Champions. My gold basketball is somewhere at the bottom of the river between Blackshear and Patterson. In my younger days when things didn't go just right, I made quick decisions before I put my brain in gear. The little gold basketball had been loaned to my girlfriend to wear and we were having a discussion in the car one evening when she decided the basketball charm meant more to me than her and handed it back. I did the only reasonly thing a teenage boy could do under the circumstances and rolled down my car window and tossed the charm into the river. It just seemed like the thing to do at the time.

Today, you can wear about anything you like and not feel out of place. The next time at Wal-Mart, stop for a moment and observe those around you and you'll see what I mean. That wasn't the case in the fifties. To feel dressed properly for boys was to have on Levi's cuffed and a short sleeve shirt with the sleeves rolled up. Shirt collar had to be up at the back. This gave you the "Elvis" look. White buck shoes and a narrow white belt dressed in a pink shirt were at the top of the style department.

Boys wore crew cut haircuts for the most part. Elvis introduced the long hair with sideburn look. It was called a ducktail. That's because it had kind of a ducky look. All slicked back and brushed to a point to the back of your head. A few brave boys at school copied the style.

Girls wore penny loafers and slacks that stopped right below the knee. They wore their dresses long with the skirts having a fluffed outlook. Ponytails became popular.

Girls could dance the jitterbug and their hair stay in place. Five and dime stores sold music on the 45-rpm record speed. Most of the time, two songs were recorded on the record. A hit song on one side and a song you never heard of on the flip side and wouldn't buy if it weren't for the hit song. It was the beginning of the creative marketer.

Senior year memories are stored away for a lifetime. Thinking back, it's the year most of us reached the top of the learning curve in knowledge and intelligence or so we thought. We were knowledgeable on anything and everything. All of a sudden, parents, teachers and coaches didn't seem to have it together like we did.

At the mature age of seventeen and eighteen, you feel like being on the top of the mountain looking down on the less knowledgeable. Thankfully, our brains finally kick back in gear and most of us continue to grow and mature and become worthwhile contributors to society.

My grades were so bad I told my children grades were not recorded that long ago. Back then, it seemed to me and a few classmates of my mentality, we had mastered the things we needed to know. I could speak English, at least the South Georgia way and figured writing was only for those who had trouble speaking. Shakespeare was some Englishman who spoke in a weird sort of way and didn't make any sense at all. Reading Zane Gray western pocketbooks were a lot more interesting.

Math was something else. Once you memorized your adding, subtracting, dividing and multiplication tables, what else did anyone really need? Pie or square and other funny looking formulas were for the weird kids, or so I thought.

It was in my first year algebra class that a learning experience occurred which has stayed with me over the years. At the beginning of the first semester, my ability to grasp and understand algebra was getting harder by the day. The teacher continued to draw equations and formulas on the board, but their meaning and how to do the work became more and more confusing. I was too shy in those days to raise my hand and ask for help. What if my classmates started giggling and made fun of me? It was a risk I couldn't afford to take.

I had decided to transfer to a basic math class and leave the algebra to others. At about this time, our algebra teacher became sick and missed about two weeks of school. A local minister in Blackshear filled in for him. Now, the minister had a different way of explaining equations and how all those algebra formulas worked. For some strange reason, I found myself understanding what it all meant.

The new teacher had a refreshing way of explaining this mumbo jumbo and all of a sudden it started making sense. My final grade will not be divulged but it was a passing score.

Later, while teaching communications as an instructor at Fort Gordon, Georgia, I often reflected back on my school days to help me remember there are no dumb kids if you take the time to reach all the students and make them feel they are important to the class. It became a rewarding experience to work with young soldiers who had a problem similar to mine and see them graduate at the top of the class.

In August 1955 I was finally a senior in high school. I seldom studied, except for basketball and recess, so it was another miracle that I made it that far. My goal of playing on the first team for the Blackshear Tigers was finally realized. Benny James had started at guard since the tenth grade. McCoy Carter and I rotated the other guard position in the eleventh grade and now that McCoy had graduated, my turn finally arrived.

McCoy was a farm boy like me with one major difference. His family was prominent farmers with a large farm, so their economic standing was somewhat different from how I grew up. His demeanor was such though that I thought he was just another son of a poor farmer. We played basketball together and McCoy was always cordial, friendly and a very talented basketball player.

Then one day in 1955, a brand new ford convertible, painted pink and white, drove up outside the basketball barn where we played our games and practiced every day. McCoy was driving. Rumors were that the shiny new car was given to him for a graduation present. The thought may have crossed my mind that it would be nice if his parents would adopt me for a month or two and buy me one.

Jackie Dixon graduated and Ferrell Dixon was the starting center. Donald and Steven Bowen were the two forwards. Both were on the first team as juniors. We were the class "A "state champions the year before. We were going to repeat as state champions, or so we thought.

The Savannah Morning News began a Christmas basketball tournament the year before and the Blackshear Tigers were invited. We didn't win the tournament in 1954 but was one of the favored teams to win as I recall. It was an honor just to be invited and Coach Childs drilled us hard to be ready to play. Anyway, the Savannah Morning News invited us back for 1955. Hinesville, Georgia high school had three giants playing on their team. I mean giants. The center was six feet nine and both forwards were six feet seven each. It was a natural assumption that they would win the tournament by the experts, whoever they were.

We knew Hinesville was good because we played them in our gym in Blackshear back in November and won the game by one basket. Three giants of that size were unheard of for high school basketball. When they warmed up before the game, three players in a row dunked the ball like it was nothing. Nobody on our team could dunk the ball, except Robert Strickland. Robert stood around five feet, nine inches tall and could jump like a jack rabbit. Our tallest player was Ferrell Dixon and he was just over six feet, two inches.

We beat Hinesville in the tournament again by the grand total of two points, which knocked them out before the championship. The championship game was against Savannah High School. It was a close game but the Tigers came out on top and won the Tournament.

At the end of the tournament, I was selected the Most Valuable Player. It was my time to do something right for a change. Playing basketball is like a lot of other things we do in life. Sometimes, everything we do appear to turn out right and sometimes everything we do appears to turn out wrong.

The coach of the basketball team at Georgia Southern was J. B. Scarce. Georgia Southern was called Georgia Teachers College back in those days. After the tournament, Coach Childs introduced me to Coach Scarce and he assured me that I would play basketball on a scholarship for his team at Georgia Teachers College when I graduated.

My dream was to go to college and play basketball at Georgia Teachers College, now renamed Georgia Southern University. Coach Childs told me that the university would grant me a four year scholarship when I graduated. He made this promise when I was selected the Most Valuable player during the Savannah Morning News Christmas basketball tournament in December, 1955.

It was a bitter disappointment when I was told that the four year scholarship was no longer on the table. The excuse I was given was they gave the scholarship to a player from a high school from Kentucky who was bigger, faster and taller than I was. Looking back to this time in my life, it was probably a blessing that I was unable to see.

Setzers Supermarket opened in downtown Waycross in October 1955. It was one of the biggest and most modern supermarkets in South Georgia. Gone were the days of giving your grocery list to the store clerk. Now all you had to do was get your grocery basket and find your groceries stacked neatly in isles. Cash registers with clerks were located at the front of the store, just like today, to check you out. It was something to watch the clerk's punch in each item purchased and ring it up. Their fingers moved so fast it was a constant blur. You could say being a cash register clerk was skilled labor. Shannon and I hired on as grocery handlers. Some called us bag boys. We had to wear white aprons and dress neat. Thankfully, ties weren't a requirement. It was a special treat to bag a full load of groceries, roll it out all the way to the parking lot, empty the groceries in the trunk of the car and if you were lucky, receive a nickel or dime tip. Our hourly wage was around fifty cents an hour plus tips so money stopped being a problem. We were rolling in money.

Every Friday afternoon and all day Saturday was a work day at Setzers. When you're eighteen and working an important job like pushing groceries out to cars in a buggy, you don't have much time to notice girls, unless it turns out to be "The" girl. All three girls were pretty but the one with the long pony tail was that girl. There was no doubt in my mind that this was the prettiest little lady God had every made, in my eyes.

Her name was Marian Hilton. She didn't know it at the time, but approximately four years later, after some strenuous persuasion on my part, she would become my wife. It took that long to sell her on the idea. We raised two beautiful daughters in our forty years of marriage. Our daughters gave us six special grandchildren; three boys and three girls. Marian battled colon cancer for over five years before her death.

Most of us can reflect back to when we committed our first rebellious act. Shannon Walker and I conspired to pull ours off while working at Setzers. Bagging groceries can get to be a drag at thirty-five cents an hour, especially when tips aren't pouring in. It was the spring of 1956. We had about six months of on the job training learning all the complicated requirements on proper grocery bagging techniques. We approached management and requested a renegotiation of our contract on wages. No deal. The management folks figured we were over paid at thirty-five cents an hour. It didn't set well not having any leverage to throw back at management. Our only course of action was to take it or leave. Leaving won out and we figured to go out in style. The supermarket did a tremendous business with customers pouring in from all over South Georgia. Saturday evenings usually was the busiest. Customers lined up with their grocery cart overloaded with groceries waiting to check out. We waited until the lines reached their peak, then removed our white aprons and walked up to the store manager and quit on the spot. It felt real good.

My future seemed bleak at the time. Going to collage was out the window and my true love gave me my walking papers. Marian decided she should date other boys so naturally my class ring was returned to me. When young couples in school break up and the ring class ring is returned, that sends the clear single that the divorce is final and they are saying in a nice way to go jump in the lake or get lost, whichever is preferred. I decided to join the Army and go as far away as Korea.

Chapter 3

U.S. Army Bound

The day after graduating from high school, I ran into a few classmates at McGregor's Drugstore located on Main Street, in Blackshear. They had joined the army prior to graduation and were waiting for their induction date with great anticipation. Joining the Army sounded like a good challenge for me so I seriously considered joining up. After a lot of soul searching and deliberation, for five seconds, I decided to join the Army.

The recruiter was a very likable fellow and said I was making a good decision, if I qualified, so I had to take some tests to find out. He mumbled something that sounded like my enlistment makes his quota for the month. The sergeant had rows of ribbons on his chest and a bunch of stripes on his sleeves. The ribbons and stripes didn't mean anything to me then. He wanted to know what type work I was interested in. Making decisions quickly even before joining up was getting complicated. I told him it didn't matter as long as I didn't have to crop tobacco.

Anyway, some multiple choice tests were administered and the recruiter said I passed with flying colors and my scores indicated being a Teletype Operator was probably my best bet for a job. Being trained as a teletype operator sounded impressive even though I had no idea what it was. He signed me up and said I could leave the next day for Jacksonville, Florida with Odie and the rest, who had already enlisted but was waiting to be sworn in. They enlisted under what was called the Buddy Plan, which promised they could stay with their friends during basic training. That is, unless the Army figured there was a shortage somewhere and they needed you somewhere else to help with their shortage. We were to find out later the Army was always having a shortage, so the buddy plan was about as reliable as a broken down car with no engine. Everyone was assigned to Ft. Campbell, Kentucky, for basic training, except for me and Terry Aldridge. Our Basic Training would be at Ft. Jackson, S.C. Time was moving faster and new things that were not taught in school were occurring daily. Maybe being an adult out on my own was not so great after all.

The next day, at noon, I told mama and daddy the good news. Their days of providing for my food, shelter and clothing was coming to an end. My joining the army was never discussed with them so they were completely surprised and somewhat shocked. This joining up was my decision without any adult help from my parents or my friends. Matter of fact, I didn't discuss it with anyone. It was time for this bird to fly away from my childhood nest provided by my parents for eighteen years.

The army-recruiting sergeant told us to pack a small bag and bring only underwear and toilet articles for our trip on the Greyhound bus ride to Jacksonville. "You will be sworn in tomorrow, he said." Mama taught me to never swear so she probably wasn't aware of the requirement to swear when taking an oath.

Our first night in Jacksonville, Florida was at a downtown hotel. Whoever owned the hotel must have had strong political connections with the Army because it was a long way from being qualified for a One Star rating. Being away from home for the first night in a strange city, in a strange building, doesn't encourage a restful night of sleep.

Morning finally arrived and all the Blackshear volunteers showed up for our swearing in. I'm sure there were a few who was wishing they were anywhere in the world but where they stood at that moment. The large room was full of new prospects waiting to take the oath. A big soldier with a loud voice walked out into the center of the room. He had ribbons on his chest and stripes on his sleeves which meant he had to be a high ranking spokesperson.

The sergeant appeared overweight with a potbelly so I figured he defiantly wasn't used to hard work or reared on a farm. He hollered again and shouted "attention". We didn't know what it meant at the time but later learned it was the army way of saying shut up and stand up straight. Everyone was told to raise his or her right hand and repeat what the other soldier who suddenly appeared in front of us said. This soldier had two silver bars on his collar and we later found out he was an officer in the grade of captain. Things didn't start off on the right foot for some in our group.

The captain kept screaming at a few to put down their left hand and raise their right hand. He told them their right hand wasn't hard to find since it was the only other hand they had. After the oath was administered, we were told to find a seat and report up front to fill out some paperwork when our name was called. My turn finally arrived and the fellow at the typewriter asked all type of questions. What was my full name, date of birth, home address, and color of eyes, weight and height? He had typed the complete form when he started on another sheet of paper.

The first question was my father's name. I told him the same as my name and he hit the ceiling! "If you have the same name as your father, stupid, then you have to be a junior and the first form I typed has to be redone". He didn't like me, I could tell. Later, we boarded a train in Jacksonville headed for Ft Jackson, South Carolina. I looked up and down the train to make sure the soldier typing out the forms in Jacksonville was not on the train. I wanted to make friends fast, but not with him. Maybe things would improve after I arrived at my new home in South Carolina.

Moving from open spaces of farm life to army barracks crammed with hundreds of strangers was a cultural shock at first. After riding all night on the train from Jacksonville to Columbia, my skinny body ached all over from lack of sleep. I was already homesick. What in the world is happening to me and why did I do what I did without thinking it through? Doubts began to creep into my mind but it was already too late to back out. Only time would tell if my decision was sound or foolish.

Growing up and leaving the comfortable surroundings provided by my parents for eighteen years was over. I was a young man and it was time I became responsible for my future.

We were greeted by a couple of sergeants dressed in starched fatigues wearing helmet liners. They acted mad and agitated at something. It was obvious from the start they were not happy to see any new recruits. Both were barking out instructions so fast no one knew what to do or at least didn't know how to do what they seemed to be asking us to do. "Line up in four columns and stand at attention. Keep your mouth shut and do as your told, recruits!" one of the sergeants kept shouting.

I'll leave out the colorful language they used. Many of these army people like to use all kinds of cuss words. If mama had heard it, she would have washed their mouths out with soap for speaking such language. I don't think a single one of us knew how to line up in four columns much less stand at attention the way they wanted it done.

The next command of "right face" made one of the sergeants almost go into hysterics. Two columns turned to the right and the other two columns turned to the left with a few just standing still playing it safe. Army life for our group was not getting a good start.

At mealtime, we lined up to get into the mess hall to eat. After a few meals, it became obvious how the name came about. Everyone lined up to be served cafeteria style. The food servers were recruits detailed for the day for what was known as kitchen police (KP) duty. KP as it was called was a dreaded extra duty all recruits pulled at some time. Meals were served on metal trays with little indentions for your individual servings. Now, since recruits who served the food in their KP capacity weren't given food-handling training, it was a common thing to have the food thrown on your tray in such a manner it resembled some sort of concoction we served our livestock on the farm. We may have been hungry entering the mess hall but lost our appetite about half way down the chow line.

Sleeping accommodations, better known as army barracks, were the old two story frame structures built during the forties for World War II soldiers. Each floor had enough room for about sixty recruits. Bunks were stacked two high and each recruit had enough space to get in and out of bed. The trick for getting any sleep at night was to be the first in bed go to sleep before all the snoring began. Otherwise, it meant staying awake most of the night listening to the fellow on each side of you try and out snore each other. At the head of the bunk up next to the wall was a single metal wall locker for each soldier. A wooden footlocker was placed at the foot of the bunk.

All issued items were required to be displayed for inspection at a moment's notice. The army had a thing for everybody doing everything the same way. They even gave it a name and called it being uniform.

The barracks had windows beside each bunk space, which provided most of the summer air conditioning. Heat was generated from a large furnace then funneled all over the barracks in metal ducts or tubing. People who loved the open exposure look were hired to design the bathroom facilities in the barracks.

Privacy wasn't in the master plan. There were eight toilets in one open room with four on each side facing each other. Shower facilities consisted of around ten showers in one open room with five on each side. It was kind of like they wanted everyone to keep an eye on each other while using the facilities. For the bashful type, it was a nightmare.

One of the things I learned early on in life is that when God made people, he designed us in such a way that we could adapt to whatever environment we found ourselves in. We just hunker down and do the best we can.

Basic training at Fort Jackson was beginning to be harder than farm work! Drill Instructors received a special thrill out of harassing everyone standing at attention in front of them. You learn quickly some standard rules of survival in basic training. They are: Keep your mouth shut and don't ever, ever volunteer for anything. It was something to see the slow learners find themselves in a constant state of harassment due to their own actions.

A favorite punishment one of our drill sergeants liked was the old "bucket drill". When he found someone out of step while marching, he would yank the recruit out of formation and make him put a bucket over his head and repeat over and over; this is my left foot, this is my right foot, this is my left foot, this is my right foot. They eventually figured it out. We were taught our rifles were called weapons. Any recruit caught calling his rifle a gun could place his own life in jeopardy! They seemed to enjoy telling us the difference between a rifle and a gun.

The primary purpose of basic training is to drill into each soldier how to follow orders and carry out a given mission. At the time, it seemed to most of us recruits their primary mission was to make our life as miserable as possible. We had to be taught to do things the "Army" way. The standard army rifle in the fifties was the M-1. It proved itself a powerful weapon for our soldiers during World War II and the Army didn't have plans to change. It was a semi-automatic rifle, which fired a clip of eight cartridges. Every soldier assembled and disassembled the weapon enough that it became second nature on what made it operate. One drill during basic was to assemble the rifle while blindfolded. It wasn't all that hard.

We were given a diagram showing the different parts of the M-l. The trick was to disassemble the weapon laying each part in a predefine position so that we knew from memory where the piece belonged. Repetition is a favorite teaching technique used by the army. Memorizing is another. To this day, I still remember my weapon serial number because I had to repeat it so many times. Motivation was another favorite tactic taught in basic.

We were strongly encouraged to do everything that the drill sergeants called the "army way". In other words, if you failed to complete an assignment which didn't meet their standards of the Army way, you were "washed back" a week to try again. Eight weeks of training was bad enough. To fail and "wash back" a week was unthinkable so the motivation factor worked for most recruits.

Payday was once a month. For a recruit like me, it meant earning the grand total of seventy-eight bucks a month. You had to line up (everything you do in the army is in a line it seems), then stand at attention and salute the pay officer with; private Gill reporting for pay, Sir. The pay officer counted off the fresh crisp bills and handed them to you. Next in line was someone taking money for your monthly laundry bill and a few more mandatory collection points before clearing the line. By the time we reached the end of the line, we were lucky to have any money left. Recruits were trapped like rats in a trap with nowhere to turn and to afraid to say anything.

The selective service was in full operation back in the fifties. Every male eighteen years of age had to register and most stood a good chance of serving their country for two years. The army was basically all male with just a handful of volunteer females. The draftees called those of us who joined up "lifers". We called them draftees and other choice names. Unless your family had an awful lot of political influence, you ended up in the United States Army for a two-year tour of duty. The Selective Service method of drafting people from every walk of life in the United States made the Army a smorgasbord of our society. Every type human being God created was in the Army. Some were highly educated from some of the finest colleges in America.

Others were drafted off the streets and in some cases, gangs from our cities and towns while for the most part; they came from the rural areas of this great country like South Georgia. Some of the new recruits spoke in strange sounding ways. Talking to someone from places like New York, Brooklyn, Pittsburgh and Boston took a lot of concentration. Their sentences ran together and they must have all been in a hurry because they all talked so fast. It wasn't uncommon to be discussing something very serious with someone from Brooklyn and all of a sudden, he would burst out laughing. It could make you self-conscious if you weren't careful.

Eight weeks of basic training in the Army consisted of marching, drilling, weapons instruction, hand to hand combat techniques, proper wearing of the uniform, military tradition, physical training, guard duty and a lot of other stuff the Army felt new recruits required to be a soldier. My eight weeks was almost up and graduation was just around the corner. Graduation meant all graduating recruits marched in formation, in their class "A's" uniform. A class "A" uniform in the summertime was fresh starched khakis with your pant sleeves tucked into your boots. You wore your tie with the end of the tie tucked inside your front shirt. Headgear consisted of a cap, which was referred to as a flying saucer.

The reviewing stand was filled with the Post Commanding officer and all his friends. They must have been the commander's friends because most were officers.

The parade drill was called "March in review". We could invite our families to attend but I elected to graduate and get the heck off base and home on leave as quickly as possible. At the time, graduation from basic training and leaving Fort Jackson, South Carolina was the happiest day of my life.

Two weeks of leave at home was coming to an end. The two weeks flew by. It was off to Fort Gordon, Georgia for advanced training in army communications. This was my first exposure to Teletype and how the Army communicated. We were taught how to type up a message on a Teletype machine and send it around the world over the army communications facilities. This was before computers so sending a message over the airways at sixty words a minute was fast.

The army takes a lot of pride in making sure its troops learn their Military Occupational Specialty (MOS) and can perform required tasks. Since the draft was in place and each class consisted of draftees and volunteers, the makeup was quite remarkable. We could have students with a PhD degree, lawyers, engineers, accountants, farmers and school dropouts, all in the same classroom.

To insure everyone could understand the military instructors, all training material was based on a ninth grade learning level. It was good for some and terribly boring for others. Typing up a message on a machine that spit out a narrow little tape with holes punched in it that could be sent through a machine to a station around the world was awesome from my point of view. There were no Teletype machines on our farm or in Blackshear that I was aware of. This was high tech and the Army was going to pay me to do it. What a deal.

My long-range goal to join the Army after graduating from High School consisted of about two seconds of preparation. I just did it. Being assigned to the Signal Corps, which is where the Army assigns its communicators, was the result of my special angel, looking out for me. Without any planning on my part, God was setting in motion the beginning of my journey of twenty three years as an army communicator. Here was an opportunity to learn new things and begin a career that was interesting plus challenging.

Going to class everyday to learn how to communicate the Army way, was no longer a boring day trying to stay awake in class, but a daily challenge to learn everything I could learn about my new job. Who knows, maybe one day in the future I would empress the pretty little girl from Waycross with the ponytail, that I could do more than walk and chew bubblegum at the same time. Gosh! Isn't it amazing how the Lord takes care of his children? We may wander around and drift away from God but He is always there to left me up and firmly plant me on my feet.

Basketball was still in my blood. Each Army post had a basketball team and since the draft was in place, it was a common occurrence to see some college all American players drafted and playing on the post team. Fort Gordon had a real good team. Tom Gola, who was an All-American center from LaSalle College and another player who played for the Harlem Globetrotters, was also on the team. I found out through the Army information grapevine there was going to be tryouts. The Army has information grapevines just like all cities and towns have.

This was in October 1956 and my orders for my next assignment were to Korea. If I could by luck make the post team and play with some outstanding players, my orders to Korea would be revoked. The only problem was students were not supposed to try out. My stubborn streak kicked in gear so I figured out a way to try out.

Playing basketball with players like All American Tom Gola from LaSalle University and a Harlem Globetrotter draftee was quite an experience. Those guys did things with a basketball that didn't seem possible. My basketball skills came up short when matched up with the talented players the coach had to choose from. My next assignment to Korea would give me another opportunity to play on an Army Post team. Playing was still in my blood.

Graduating from the Signal School was a special day. My oldest sister Thelma came with mama and daddy for the ceremony. My family knew I would be leaving the next day for a sixteen month tour of duty in Korea. There were others in my graduating class that would be going along for the long airplane ride across country to Ft. Lewis, Washington.

Our company commander posed a notice that all graduation students departing Ft. Gordon the next day, was restricted to barracks for the night. He didn't want to take the chance of soldiers getting in trouble their last night on base and possibly ruining his career. That decision didn't set well with me and two other classmates leaving for Korea. It wasn't right and besides, what could they do to us if we disobeyed his orders? We soon found out.

There was a good movie playing at the post theatre and the thought of having a nice salty bag of popcorn with a coke won out over hanging out at the barracks until bedtime with nothing to do.

We slipped out of the area and headed for the theatre. We had to slip out because the commander had posted lookouts to catch anyone trying to skip out.

When the movie ended, the three of us headed back to our barracks area to slip back in like we slipped out. Suddenly, someone shouted, "hold it right where you are and hit the ground." After we skipped out, the commander held a roll call so he knew we left the area and was waiting for us when we got back.

The army tries to maintain the cleanest eating facilities possible, especially the floors. We spent the rest of the night with a toothbrush in each hand, scrubbing the floor in the mess hall. It was a bitter way to learn the consequences of disobeying orders.

Chapter 4

Korea

The Army bus drove us from Fort Gordon to the airfield in Augusta, Georgia. Sixteen from my Communications class were on the bus headed for our next assignment, which was destination Korea. A DC-3 two engine aircraft was on the ramp waiting for our arrival. Tiger Airlines in bold print was on the fuselage. It probably was some special combat plane to be named Tiger Airlines.

After boarding the aircraft, an unfriendly stewardess with what appeared to be two little red horns on her head, tossed out wool army blankets to all the soldiers. Unfriendly people always appear ugly in appearance for some reason. She shouted out something like we might need them before we reached Ft. Lewis, Washington and was right. We almost froze to death on that DC-3. My flying experience was non-existent at the time so I just figured that was the way flying was supposed to be. It was a long, boring trip. We were not flying all that high and glimpses of the countryside could be observed out the window.

During the flight, the pilot landed at an airport somewhere in Idaho. The stewardess announced that it was a refueling stop and our time on the ground would be less than an hour. The weather was freezing cold with a mixture of snow and sleet falling at a rapid pace. After the gas tanks on the plane were full and the fuel trucks pulled away, another truck appeared and began spraying the aircraft, they were de-icing the plane so that ice would not accumulate on the wings. Ice on airplane wings does not make a good combination

Flying on a cold, noisy airplane at around 180 knots, made our venture across country long and weary. Finally, Ft. Lewis was a welcome site.

A plane load of tired, sleepy soldiers exited the DC-3 and boarded buses for a short ride to the Army processing center. After two weeks of processing, we embarked for the troop ship docked in Seattle, Washington, waiting to take us to our next duty station, Korea.

Army processing centers are world renowned for making recruits practice hurry up and wait tactics until it is a fine tuned art. Hurry up and wait drills were done almost every hour of every day until we boarded busses again for the ride to Seattle, Washington, where an old World War II troop ship was waiting to haul over two thousand soldiers to Korea.

One special memory of Seattle, Washington, was spending a Sunday at the home of one of our classmates from Seattle. After fifty-four years have passed, I can't recall his name but he invited me to his home. We went to church and then had a delicious home cooked meal prepared by his mom. It made a lasting impression on me to know there were good people all over the world.

The USS Patrick was a troop ship capable of hauling over 2,000 soldiers. Once everyone who was headed for Korea boarded, it seemed to me the transportation folks crammed about 2500 on a ship built for no more than 2000. My accommodations were exactly like everyone else; a canvas rack stacked five high. There was just enough room to slide into the rack for sleeping purposes. Duffle bags with all our worldly military belongings were hung on a pole at the head of each rack.

The voyage across the Pacific Ocean took twenty-one days. The routine for twenty-one long and boring days was the same each day. Wake up at six a.m., then try and take a shower if you could with the ship rolling from side to side. Next was to line up for breakfast, eat, line up for lunch, and eat then line up for dinner. The next day the same drill was completed. We became so proficient the ship captain let us do the drill every single day during the complete voyage.

There were movies shown on deck if the weather permitted and you were lucky enough to find a spot to stand or sit, which helped pass the time. The Navy crew kept a chart on deck, which showed the ships position each day. The line showing daily progress seemed to creep along. A lot of soldiers became seasick from the constant up and down motion ships make when crossing oceans. Waiting in a long chow line and watching troops throw up does not make a good combination or a hungry appetite.

Traveling at a speed of twenty knots with nothing to see but water everywhere can become monotonous. It was a welcome sight the morning we awoke to see the shoreline of Korea. We saw snow on the mountains overlooking Inchon harbor. It was late November 1956 and for a young man raised in South Georgia; the weather was extremely cold, damp and freezing. Our troop ship dropped anchor in Inchon Bay. We were offloaded on barges for the short trip to shore. Barges had to be used because the water in the bay was not deep enough for the troop ship to tie up to the dock.

The Korean War came to a stalemate in 1953 but the remnants of war were still present from the scars of battle. It was my first experience in seeing a foreign land where Americans fought and died for our freedom. If you are looking to see a hero, please go to any military cemetery. They gave their lives so that we may live in a country as free men and women.

For this nineteen year old at the time, it has had a lasting impression on me. There were thousands called to active duty to serve this great country during the Korean War. Many were from our own families. Others were friends like my former Sunday school teacher Pete Peterson who served his country in Korea with honor as an infantryman. You don't ever hear these men and women talk about the sacrifices required from them but they all served our country proudly. It's what others have done on our behalf that makes our eyes moist up with tears and our voices choke up when we hear the beautiful song, God Bless America.

My home in Korea for the next sixteen months would be adjacent to a small village called Ouijungbu. I was assigned to the 51st Signal Battalion. Our living quarters were metal Quonset huts. There were approximately twenty to thirty soldiers in each hut. Two pot-bellied diesel-burning stoves provided heat. In the summer time, opening the doors at each end of the Quonset and raising all the windows produced the air conditioning. If you were real smart, you stayed outside and away from the hut until it was absolutely bedtime.

Each Quonset hut had a Korean houseboy assigned for housekeeping to include shining boots and making up bunks and washing dirty uniforms. What a break! We chipped in about two bucks a piece for his salary, which was a good paying job for a South Korean at that time. Our houseboy was called Kim but then, about two thirds of all Koreans were named Kim it seemed. Koreans favorite food was called kimchi. Kimchi was fermented vegetables fixed a special way that only a person raised in Korea could produce. The aroma smelled like rotten vegetables or that's what it smelled like to me. I never got up enough nerve to see how it tasted. Those that did said it was delicious but then, who knows what they drank while dining on a Korean meal?

The 51st Signal Battalion provided communications for the Army's I Corps headquarters. My job was to work in the Communications Center as a Teletype operator. We had Teletype circuits to all the divisions, Corps artillery, and Eighth Army headquarters located outside Seoul, Korea. This was my first experience working shift work. Communications centers are manned twenty-four hours a day so we all rotated back and forth on different shits.

This was also my first exposure to cryptography. Now don't confuse crypto with that stuff that caused Superman so much heartache. Cryptography, which was shortened to Crypto, is the method used to keep messages secret. A typical teletype message that was classified would be encrypted using a cryptographic machine. To read the message you had to have the code. Everyone else saw a message tape with a bunch of scrambled letters and characters that made no sense.

The Army didn't allow just anyone to handle classified messages. We had to have back ground checks completed to make sure we were nice, trustworthy soldiers. A security clearance authorizing the handling of Confidential and Secret material was then issued. To obtain a Top Secret clearance, the FBI was required to conduct background checks, which took longer and was much more through to double check that we could be trusted to safeguard military secrets. There wasn't a big demand for spying back in South Georgia, so I passed the clearance requirements easily.

My first few weeks in Korea were remarkable only in that I survived. It was my first experience being in another country and not knowing a single soul from South Georgia didn't help. I've always enjoyed reading and spent many an hour at the base library reading books, mostly history. On this particular day, a young officer approached me in the library and wanted to know if I was from Blackshear, Georgia. His name was John Fesperman. John was a First Lieutenant stationed at headquarters of the 51st Signal Battalion. He happened to notice my name on the ship manifest that I arrived on, and had looked me up. Although we didn't know each other at the time, we have remained friends over the years. It sure did brighten up my day to find someone from South Georgia. Unfortunately for me, John's tour of duty was coming to an end and he rotated back to the states shortly thereafter.

My first year in Korea had almost rolled around. It was late October 1957 when a notice in the local edition of the Stars and Stripes newspaper advised of basketball tryouts for the I Corps team. Teletype and crypto was neat stuff but playing basketball everyday would be a lot better. Coach Childs must have brain washed me in high school because I still wanted to play basketball. Who knows, maybe all the All-American draftees stayed in the United States and I would have a shot at making the team. Anyway, I was still in good shape at age twenty and army chow had added some weight to my six-foot frame.

I had overcome my one night of stupidity drinking vodka and lucked out by making the team. It seemed to me back then that there were a lot of players with more talent than I on our team but by working a little harder and staying in better physical condition, my performance was at least good enough to make the first team. It was another one of the learning experience we pick up as we travel down the road of life; we tend to get out of things that we put in. Use your God given talents to do the best of your ability and life will be rewarding. Try doing things the easy way and not at your best will not be fulfilling. Hard work and trying to do your best had been instilled in me by my parents and many of my teachers. It paid off then and is still paying off.

My tour of duty in Korea was coming to an end. Sixteen months away from home stationed in a desolate place called Korea was almost finished. My new orders assigning me to Fort McClellan, Alabama had arrived and all that was lacking was my port call. We could request to fly back on a military cargo aircraft but in early 1958, troop passenger ships like the one I came over on was the primary means of transportation. My flying experience on the Flying Tiger airlines from Fort Gordon to ft. Lewis, Washington wasn't all that memorable so I didn't attempt to fly back. I figured twenty-one days on a troop ship like I came over on would be a piece of cake now that I was a seasoned sailor with one long voyage under my belt. Not surprisingly, the events coming back to the United States was almost the same as going over. Actually, it was twenty-three days on the return trip. The ship must have had a smaller engine or something. Boy was I glad I joined the Army and not the Navy.

It was a beautiful site to look out over the horizon and see the first glimpse of land as our ship approached the harbor of San Francisco, California. The army tugboats met our ship in the harbor and escorted us under the Golden Gate Bridge. The good old United States of America was one beautiful site.

After clearing all the Army red tape of processing at the Oakland Army Terminal, I was on my way to the greyhound bus station to buy a ticket to Waycross, Georgia. See the USA in a Chevrolet would have been nice but with no car, my next choice was a Greyhound bus. I had three weeks of leave time before checking in at my next assignment at Fort McClellan, Alabama. It took three days and two nights for the trip home, but when you're twenty years of age, a little bus ride is nothing.

I saw a lot more of the American landscape from the window of a bus than the window of an airplane so the trip was long but well worth the drive. Riding on a bus through California, Nevada, Arizona, New Mexico, Texas, Louisiana, Mississippi, and Alabama is a wonderful experience. When God made America, he made the most beautiful country in the world. Each state has its own unique features but it's hard to beat my home state of Georgia. It makes calling Waycross and Blackshear home that much more special. Besides, we all speak the same easygoing way and without an accent like the Northern folks have.

Fort McClellan, Alabama was the home of the Army Chemical Corps. My job was in Communications Center Operations as a Teletype operator. The Army must have some kind of secret plans for me to be going to a Chemical post. Nope! It's what is called in army lingo being mal-assigned. In other words, you were sent to a company where there was no chance of working in what you were trained to do. The closest job they found at McClellan for me was working in the Supply room doing typing and paperwork. It didn't matter to me though; every chance I got was hitching a ride back and forth to Waycross and Blackshear. Fort McClellan had a post basketball team and with the experience picked up playing on the I Corps team in Korea, my expectations were all positive on making the team. What a life, I thought.

Hitch hiking a ride home was beginning to be a drag. Most of the time, nice folks would stop and give a soldier a ride but there was always the exception. On a couple of occasions, some rednecks or roughnecks they thought, would try and intimidate you after giving you a ride. In most cases, it was young men who had too much alcohol to drink and felt they needed to impress someone. It was time to stop pressing my luck and buy some sort of transportation.

My first car was a two tone yellow and white 1956 Ford Fairlane. It was approximately two years old and cost nine hundred dollars. What a beauty! It had two doors and an eight cylinder engine; around 350 horsepower with an automatic transmission. The dashboard was dark gray and padded for safety. This was before seatbelts so all that stood between you and the glass wraparound windshield was the padded dash. Safety just didn't seem all that important back in the fifties when driving a car.

My ford Fairlane had a built-in AM (Amplitude Modulation) radio stations were the only type broadcasting in Waycross and the surrounding area when I was growing up. In Waycross, we could pick up stations WAYX and WACL. Nighttime was different. All kinds of AM stations would pop up. AM signals bounce up and down sort of like a bouncing rubber ball and they must love the night air because they bounce so much further and clearer.

The first FM (Frequency Modulated) Radio Station appeared in late 1937. It would be over thirty years before an FM station became operational in Waycross or Blackshear.

Chapter 5

Falling in Love

Now that I had my own car, every spare weekend was spent driving to Waycross. Marian, who I met while working at Setzers in 1955, was now graduated from High School and working as a Dental Assistant for Doctor Wink Lee. She dated a lot back then but not with me. I wanted to scream and pull my hair out when she said things like we should stay in touch because I was such a dear friend. Bull! There had to be some way of letting her know that she was someone very special in my life and I wasn't referring to being good friends either. Young men can't go around telling girls how they really feel about them because there is always the chance they'll tell you to get lost, bug out or go jump in a lake. Every man has his pride!

I was fortunate to have made the Fort McClellan basketball team and we were starting to make a lot of road trips to other bases. It was January, 1959 when we set out for a trip to the Marine Corps Supply Base in Albany, Georgia, Moody Air Force Base in Valdosta, then off to Fort Gordon, Georgia; Shaw Air Force Base in South Carolina and a loop back to the Naval Air Station in Jacksonville, Florida. I made a point of letting Marian know when we would be at Moody Air Force base. She took the bait and with her best friend Marie Griffin, traveled to Moody to see us play.

My game plan called for me to be nonchalant about the whole thing and even dropped quite a few hints that I could hardly wait to get back to Fort McClellan to see a young lady I had recently met. The meeting a young girl in Alabama was true but I must confess, highly exaggerated. This was my way of keeping her informed and because she said herself what a good friend I was to her, it was only fitting that she be kept informed on new friends in my life . . . It worked. It was about three weeks before we completed the road trip and returned to Fort McClellan.

A letter from Marian was waiting for me. It was written and mailed the day after our game at Moody AFB. She let me know in the special way she had of saying things when upset, like she didn't appreciate driving all the way to Valdosta to see me and then have to put up with all I could talk about was some girl named Joyce, in Alabama. The truth of the matter was I had met a girl named Joyce but we had not dated.

That night, at a pay phone on the base, I called her to let her know I was back at Fort McClellan and had read her letter. She had a way of winning most of our arguments and to the best of my knowledge; she was winning this argument when I said if she was that upset, then why not marry me! Is there a more romantic way to purpose to the girl you love . . . it worked! She said yes. Asking someone you love to be your wife is a bold move for a twenty-one year old. I bought the engagement and wedding rings at Harts Jewelry store in Waycross the next weekend. We were at the US #1 drive-in theatre when I presented her the engagement ring. There isn't a more romantic setting than a drive-in theatre to present the girl of your dreams a wedding ring. No matter how hard I try, the name of the movie playing that night remains a mystery.

Looking back on how all this played out seems lacking a lot on my part for being so unromantic. Marian must have seen something in me that even I had not seen up to that time in our lives. We were married August 2, 1959 at Central Baptist Church, in Waycross. It was the happiest day of my life.

My military rank when Marian and I were married was Specialist Fourth Class, which is the same as an enlisted E-4. My total gross pay to include quarters and ration allowance was $278.00 a month. The monthly tax withholdings aren't so bad when you're in the less than three hundred bucks a month tax bracket. Our rent for a one bedroom furnished apartment was $68.00. We still had an electric, garbage and water bill, which put a big dent in my enormous paycheck. Grocery shopping was done on base at the base commissary.

A commissary is the Army discount grocery store on post. Military families could purchase their groceries at cost, or so they said. It was somewhat cheaper than the downtown stores but at claiming it was at cost was a stretch.

We couldn't afford a telephone and didn't have to worry about being able to afford a computer, color TV, VCR, tape deck or camcorder because they had not been invented. Through the magic of practical grocery shopping, Marian bought our monthly supply of food with a twenty-dollar bill. She had a big influence on recipes that went in the cookbook, "how to prepare hamburger 100 different ways." Hamburger meat was 4 pounds for a buck. A gallon of gas was twenty-nine cents. We treated ourselves once a month to eating out on payday. Our favorite was a diner on US highway One that served a complete meal for ninety-nine cents. The income wasn't so great back then but the output wasn't so bad either.

Washing clothes was done at a local self-help laundry facility. All you needed was some detergent and a bunch of quarters. Watching a black and white TV provided most of the nightly entertainment, or playing pinochle with your neighbors who were in the same financial boat as you. Our military friends had the same amount of money as we did so we couldn't pass the hat for relief.

Chapter 6

Military instructor

Playing basketball was still in my system when Marian and I married. It was a lot of fun to go on road trips to other bases and have my wife travel along with me. Her job on the road trips was to record game statics. It was in the fall of 1960 when we departed Fort Gordon for a series of games at Fort Jackson, S.C., Shaw Air Force Base, S.C. then back to Moody Air Force base and on to Jacksonville, Florida to play at the Naval Air Station. We were paid a few extra bucks for expense money, which the Army calls per-diem. It helped out because I was still an E-4 and no chance of a promotion while playing basketball.

It was around this time when it suddenly dawned on me that it was time to stop the game playing and to get on with life for myself and my family. Who knows, there might be two baby girls to take care of later on.

After basketball season ended and we were sent back to our units to work in our normal military jobs, I was selected to attend a three-week course of instruction on how to be a military instructor. Somebody up the chain of command must have thought I could explain this communications stuff to other recruits. It was very refreshing to go to class for three weeks and learn the mechanics of teaching in front of a classroom full of students.

There were two instructors who taught the class proper teaching techniques on how to be an effective military instructor. Both were drafted into the Army from their civilian teaching careers. They did a fine job of teaching about fifteen classmates the finer points on how to be a good military instructor. Before we could graduate and be certified as a qualified instructor, each student was required to teach three different subjects in five, ten and fifteen minute time periods. We were assigned what subject to teach and then had to write our own lesson plans accordingly. Every student would be graded on posture, delivery, how to ask a question, eye contact, subject matter and a lot of other things that I don't remember. Standing in front of a group of people for the first time causes a feeling in the pit of your stomach to feel like a bunch of churning butterflies. I've heard that if the churning butterfly feeling is missing, then the audience is in for a boring speech.

My first assignment as a Communications Instructor was teaching Teletype Operating Procedures. The course was eight weeks long and if a soldier stayed awake through half the classes, he or she would have a pretty good understanding of Teletype operations. Sleeping in class really wasn't allowed and we had our own special way to motivate students who tended to take like cat naps during class. It was in the spring of 1961 when my assignment as an instructor began. My grade was still Specialist, E-4. Marian was pregnant with our first child and I was trying everything possible to move up in grade so that we could relax a little bit and not be so stretched from pay day to pay day. There were months when it appeared the incoming funds would fall short on matching the outgoing funds.

To be promoted, enlisted troops had to pass advancement tests and go before promotion boards to move a notch on the pass ladder. Marian was a good sport and drilled me nightly on what we hoped was the right material to study for the test and to prepare for the promotion board. Many years later we both chuckled at the memories of our first years together. We could still remember the questions and answers we practiced night after night.

The preparation paid off and I was promoted to Sergeant prior to our first child being born. Buying material things on credit was catching on all over the country. The merits of buy now, pay later, was pitched in radio and television commercials continuously, with the good executives at Sears and Roebuck leading the revolution. We opened our first charge account and purchased a baby crib for our baby, which was due at any time.

Chapter 7

Welcome home Juliann

On October 8, 1961 Marian told me in no uncertain terms that it was time to drive her to the Fort Gordon hospital. Labor pains were coming at a faster pace and we lived a good thirty minutes from the hospital. A slight breeze was blowing which helped somewhat because the weather was still warm for early October. We loaded up our little rear engine Renault and took off immediately for the hospital. There are a lot of things I've had to do over the years but delivering a baby was not something I wanted to do.

The base hospital in 1961 was the old frame, single story building, constructed for use by World War II soldiers. Each wing in the hospital was connected by an enclosed walkway. A lot of time was spent walking down the long hospital walkways connecting all the buildings together. Supposedly, the facility was constructed so that in the event of fire, it could be contained between each wing. Although the buildings were old, the Army took pride in keeping all the linoleum floors clean and highly buffed. Manpower was plentiful and a few privates were always available to do the cleaning choirs.

The nurse met us at the reception desk and escorted Marian to the delivery ward. I was told to wait next door in the waiting lounge. There hadn't been any pregnancy problems so I had a seat and waited for the good news. This was something. My wife was giving birth to our first child. I would be a father. Nobody bothered back then tried to figure out in advance if it was a boy or girl, or at least we didn't. We just wanted a healthy, beautiful baby. We could care less if it was a boy or girl I was a twenty-four year old cool, laid back, almost dad, or so I thought. My only problem was the room seemed awful warm.

The Army has its own methodical way of doing things. Even though the outside temperature was in the seventies, the hospital heating system had been turned on. October is supposed to be cold so all heating systems were on the go. Outside temperature just didn't matter. It had to be the heat that caused what happened to me next.

I was sitting on a couch in the lounge when the nurse stuck her head in the door. She smiled and said congratulations; I was the father of a beautiful baby girl. She also said that I could follow her to the delivery room to see Marian and the baby. I popped up off the coach, took about two steps and fainted. When I woke up, the nurse was holding ammonia under my noise and helping me to my feet. They were gracious enough to help hold me up when I entered the room to see Marian and our brand new baby daughter, Sarah Juliann; I took a lot of ribbing caused by my little insignificant fainting spell. It had to be caused from the excess heat. Soldiers don't pass out. I had never fainted in my life and would not again, until our next daughter was born.

It is amazing how a small, precious little baby can change two parents' lives so drastically in such a short time. What a boring life we must have lived because about everything we did now evolved around Juliann.

Babies require a lot of attention and have their own special way of insuring that mom and dad take note. I never figured out how she did it, but Marian could tell from the sound of Juliann's cry whether she was hungry, had a wet diaper or the other type, or just wanted some attention. All the cry sounds sounded the same to me. All the noise from target practice in basic firing the M-1 probably had affected my hearing.

It always made Marian awfully mad but there were times when she would say something to me and I wouldn't hear a thing. Like, "It's your turn to rock her. Don't just sit there; I know you can hear her crying!" Wives just didn't appreciate all the sacrifices we made training to be the best soldier we could be.

In April 1962, I was promoted to Staff Sergeant E-6. My grade as an Instructor called for a soldier in the grade of E-6 so my superiors felt that my teaching performance warranted another shot at being promoted. Being promoted from E-4 to an E-6 in eleven months provided much needed income now that we were three members in our family. Playing basketball for the Army was a lot of fun but I found out hard work just like on the farm proved to be the most rewarding. It also helped financially and professionally. You tend to find something always being needed for a new baby in the family.

In May 1962, I was sent on special duty to assist in field-testing a new Communication System being conducted at Fort Gordon by Minneapolis Honeywell Corp. The Semi-Automatic Message Distribution System was designed for the army communications center at the pentagon in Washington, D.C. Teletype messages sent and received at the Pentagon were currently being handled manually and—this new system was designed and manufactured to expedite the message handling in the Pentagon. Teaching students Teletype procedures had been fun and challenging, but testing new fangled systems before anybody else had a look, sounded even more interesting.

The electronic equipment filled up a building about the size of a three-bedroom house. Honeywell filled most of the room with racks of printed circuit boards they designed. It was my first exposure to the technical side of communications. The civilian engineers who worked for Honeywell spoke their on technical language. It was only a matter of time before such things as conductors, transistors, resistors and flip-flop circuits outlined on a schematic diagram were just another way of talking. A console with four monitoring positions and a slew of flashing colored lights would be the control center that processed all incoming and outgoing teletype traffic. All army teletype circuits at the Pentagon would be routed through this fancy system and four army officers in the grade of major or above could accomplish what one hundred people were currently doing. That was one of many specifications Honeywell was required to incorporate into the system.

My boss must have figured I had a way with words and assigned me the task of writing up the procedures on how the darn thing would operate. This assignment was my first shot ever of having to write a complete sentence. I had to learn how to write field manuals the army way. The first requirement was to insure that the subject matter was written in a dry, humdrum, uninteresting manner and what I produced probably won some type award for being dry and uninteresting. Anyway, it dawned on me that to be able to write a manual on how the system operated what buttons to push to make it work, required some kind of idea on how their present system operated.

This would entail a trip to Washington D.C to visit the Communications Center at the Pentagon. Traveling orders, which the army calls temporary duty or TDY for short, were issued for my three-day trip.

Boarding a train in Augusta, Georgia and riding all night in a Pullman was a neat way to travel. It was my first experience trying to sleep on a train, in a bed with so little room a small size midget would have been cramped. Riding the rails as they say in railway language is something else.

Trains tend to sway back and forth on the tracks for some reason. It became very obvious when you wake up from the josh ling back and forth and can't get back to sleep that it's somewhat different than sleeping in your bed back home.

Two well-dressed men in expensive suits met me in the office at the Pentagon where I was told to report. They were army civilians who were assigned to monitor the progress of the tests at Fort Gordon on the new system. They were both awfully friendly and treated me to lunch and showed me around the Pentagon. They kept asking me questions like didn't I feel like the Semi-Automatic Message Distribution System was going to be a complete failure and some other pointed questions. It turned out to be my first exposure to the interesting world of end fighting, politics and political persuasion.

I was only twenty-four years old but my mama and daddy didn't raise an idiot. They were trying to use me to make statements they could use to try and sabotage the complete project. The next morning I was asked if I had time to brief a few people from their department and maybe answer a few of their questions. High ranking civilian government employees asking a young Army sergeant if he had time to brief generals and colonels was probably a trick question so I played along and said I sure did.

The briefing turned out to be a room full of colonels, one general and civilians wearing expensive suits. I was dressed in my class "A" military uniform wearing my sergeant stripes. It took me a few minutes to run down how the system operated and answer a few questions. The first question asked was, "sergeant Gill, now that you've spent a few months testing this new system, isn't it your conclusion the system is not reliable and not capable of replacing our present system". Now, I didn't have to reflect too long on a question asked in that manner to figure out these folks were not interested in what I thought, but what they could get me to say that reflected their views. My answer probably sounded something like this.

"The semi-automatic message distribution system was designed to speed up message handling at the Pentagon with fewer personnel. Our testing is still ongoing so the results are still down the road."

I went on to explain that, "The actual capabilities of the system will be determined by how the system operates under vigorous test modes to determine if the input material are properly distributed as designed by the systems engineer. We will be using empirical data in our test base to insure that the outcome of the input will coincide with the army's test requirements."

I figured if they could come up with what all that meant I was home free. Thank the Lord for two instructors who thought me and others how to think clearly standing in front of a audience and do it without becoming brain-dead.

Upon returning back to Fort Gordon, I wrote my report and briefed my boss on how the folks in the Pentagon tried their best to get me to say the system was a complete flop. It was much later that I found out my boss was aware of the infighting all along and decided it was better to see me bleeding from stab wounds, so to speak, than he.

That's why he was glad to see me go on the trip . . . sometimes it's hard to recognize your friends from your enemies. Isn't it great to know that Jesus is our friend and loves us the same all the time and is always available no matter how far we drift away from Him.

Chapter 8

Germany

Military personnel become adept at being uprooted frequently for new duty stations. My turn for an overseas assignment had arrived. I was Germany bound and my wife and daughter would remain in the states for the immediate future. Army rules said government housing must be available before they would ship family and furniture. It may be two months separation from my family or it could be four, five, or up to a year of waiting. When you've elected a military career, you learn to salute and move out as ordered. It wasn't uncommon to hear a few insensitive morons state that if the Army felt you needed a family they would have issued you one.

Pack up and move out was the only legal option on the table. It was the middle of November 1962. Marian drove me to the train depot in Waycross to board a train for Philadelphia, Pennsylvania. My orders called for me to fly from Philadelphia to Rheine Main Air Force Base, Germany. Juliann was fourteen months old. She was already walking like an adult and talking up a storm. My heart broke when I overheard her asking Marian where was Daddy going and why couldn't they go with me. The memory of giving them a big hug before boarding the train will be with me forever. Having a lump in the throat and being all choked up from leaving your family would become a common occurrence during my twenty-three years of military service.

My assignment in Germany was with the 97th Signal Battalion stationed at Boebligen, Germany. I was assigned to Company C which was responsible for manning the Seventh Army Communications Center located in Vaihingen, Germany; about five miles north of Boebligen. This would be my first assignment as a Platoon Sergeant responsible for over thirty trained Army Communicators.

My boss was a Second Lieutenant who had been in the Army about three months. He was probably saying to himself how fortunate to have a well-seasoned Staff Sergeant to take care of supervising the everyday duties required of our platoon. Going from an E-4 to E-6 in eleven months at the Signal School in Fort Gordon, Georgia was great for pay purposes. It didn't help at all in training me how to be a supervisor and Leader of men. Here I was assigned the task of providing leadership and supervision for over thirty men and I had no idea on how to carry it off! Teaching soldiers how to communicate is one thing. Providing supervision and leadership is quite another.

My boss was in worse shape than me in knowing how to be a successful leader. He had been trained during his Reserve Officer Training, and I'm sure told that he would always have a well-seasoned and trained Army Sergeant to take care of the everyday activities of supervising a platoon. I was twenty-five years old; in a foreign country without my family and given an assignment I didn't have the foggiest idea on how to accomplish. Talk about the blind leading the blind.

My next year was the roughest, heart wrenching, and stressful in my life. Thankfully, a senior sergeant in the Battalion saw my predicament and provided much help and encouragement to see me through many trials and tribulations. God was there to reach down and take my failures and weak points and turn them into what would later prove to be my strongest strengths.

Winter had set in and the ground was covered with a heavy snow. Germany is a beautiful country and the German people take pride in keeping it spotless. They must have a law that says you will be taken outside and shot by a firing squad if you throw any litter on the ground. Trash on the streets or on the side of their highways is nonexistent. Driving a car on the German highway expressways, which the Germans call autobahns, is a new experience. No speed limits! Put the pedal to the metal and move out. It's how they drive.

Christmas and the New Year 1963 had begun. Two months without my wife and daughter seemed like two years. It was the first week in February when Marian wrote me a letter telling me she had received her port call which was the date she and Juliann were to report to Charleston Air Force Base to catch a chartered flight to Germany. The news caught me off guard in that the Army housing folks said it would be a least five months waiting. She gave me their arrival date at Rheine Main AFB Germany, which was only two weeks away. I required Post Housing and fast.

When I arrived early the next morning at Post Housing, the room was full of soldiers waiting to find out the status of their housing request. I soon found out that somebody back in the states had goofed and sent out port call orders premature. A planeload of dependents was already on their way and no housing was available. Well, my special angle stepped in again and saved the day for me.

The Post Sergeant Major, who is the highest-ranking enlisted person on post, stormed into the waiting room and immediately started berating the housing officials because his wife was also on the plane and he didn't have housing. Now, nobody messes around with Sergeant majors. He was screaming something like, if you don't have me housing shortly, I will have the Post Commanding General, who is a two star general and my boss, fire everyone in this office. It only took a matter of minutes to find housing for him. On his way out the office, the Sergeant Major wheeled around and told the housing folks just how incompetent they all where and then he did a strange thing.

He pointed to me setting right at the door and said to the housing officials; "What about this soldier? His family is also on the plane and they need housing. It's a disgrace what you are doing to these people"

The soldier behind the counter motioned for me to come forward. He signed me up for permanent housing immediately. They thought I was with the Sergeant Major and was taking care of me also. I had never laid eyes on the man. When Marian and Juliann arrived, we moved immediately into permanent housing without having to stay in temporary housing, which was the normal practice. Thank you Lord! I know my assigned angel was getting a workout.

Marian and Juliann arrived in Germany around the last week of February, 1963. Post housing was four story apartment buildings with sixteen families in each building. Our apartment was on the second floor. It had one bath, a kitchen, dinette area, living room and two bedrooms. All of the apartments were furnished. Since our household goods of clothing, dishes and other small items were being shipped, we made arrangements to borrow these items from Post Housing until our stuff arrived. The furniture was in good shape but style and shape was not something most reasonable families would have bought.

The couch and chairs in the living room were the overstuffed type and if by chance you dropped a quarter in the chair to see if it would bounce, it wouldn't. The Army probably wanted to make sure nobody got to comfortable and damage their property.

Chapter 9

Welcome home Elizabeth

Our second daughter was born December 1, 1963. Jesus knew Juliann needed a little sister. For some reason, Elizabeth was born nine months after her mother and sister arrived in Germany. It was in the middle of the night when Marian woke me with the news it was time to go to the hospital. Her labor pains were coming about five minutes apart and that meant to move out. Besides, there was ice and snow on the roads and the Post hospital was a good twenty-five minutes away. Fortunately, at three o'clock in the morning, traffic is slow. Our family car was a French Renault. It was a little thing with the motor in the back like a Volkswagen. My driving must have gotten a little reckless because Marian kept telling me to slow down and not kill us all. She hated the snow and never gave me the feeling of complete confidence when I was driving in snowy conditions.

Marian's doctor had led us to believe that the baby would be a boy. It had something to do with the sound and strength of the heartbeat. There were no ultra sounds back then or if they were, it was being kept hush, hush from me. Anyway, when the nurse game in and told me the good news in the waiting room that it was a beautiful baby girl, I did what I tend to do when babies arrive in our family, I fainted! I couldn't blame it on the heat. This time I'm sure it was probably caused from all the snow and ice on the roads to the hospital. Driving your wife to the hospital, which is ready to deliver a baby at any moment, is a very stressful experience. The fact we were in a foreign country didn't matters either.

Beth was a good baby. She was just as beautiful as her sister. Juliann required a lot of special attention when she was a baby but Beth tended to take everything in stride. She took her normal baby naps and at our bedtime, would sleep most of the night without waking up for attention. It probably was because she had an older sister to help out and look after her. Juliann liked to get next to the crib and just sat there and stare at her sister. Beth started crawling around nine months old and the two of them loved to chase each other throughout the apartment.

Beth was one of the fasted baby crawlers around. Her crawling capabilities were so remarkable that she decided to wait until around thirteen months to get up off the floor and walk. Beth started talking baby talk at around thirteen months also. Two syllable words gave Beth some trouble at first. She loved pickles and would ask for it by saying "I want a loudel, loudel". Marian set her down one day and said, "Beth, watch my mouth. Say "pic". Beth would say pic. Now say, "kles". Beth would say, "kles". Now say "pic-kles". Beth looked her Mom straight in the eye and said "Loudel, loudel" She took her sweet time in talking back then but has tended to make up for it in her adult life.

Sometimes when Beth comes over to the house today, I have to tell her to slow down and take a deep breath and don't forget to breathe. It was probably caused from keeping all those words bottled up when she was a baby.

At birth, Beth was born with a large birthmark on her right shoulder. It was big as a silver dollar. We were concerned about how it would look when she grew up and what affect it may have on her. The doctors advised that having it surgically removed could be dangerous. Today, there is hardly a trace of the birthmark. The good Lord just did his magic and removed it without any help from anybody.

It was only about a five-minute walk from our apartment to the Signal Company I was assigned to. Coming home for lunch was a daily routine and Juliann was normally at the stairway entrance to greet me. Beth was still just a baby. A German delivery truck make the rounds to all the Post housing units every day with German rolls called Brotchen, and all sorts of sweets. It was during our tour in Germany that Juliann and Beth got hooked on gummy bears.

This was a special treat for Juliann when she was a little girl. When I came home for lunch, I always gave her a dime to buy a bag of gummy bears. She was over two years old and probably thought she was an adult. Meeting me at the stairwell entrance to our apartment had been going on for a few weeks when Juliann's little secret was exposed.

It seems she would hit her mother up for a dime and then go downstairs and wait for my arrival and ask for another dime.

This all surfaced one day when I was looking for something and checked the small drawers located in the cabinet in the apartment vestibule. In the drawer were a handful of dimes. Juliann was hitting her mother up for a dime and then running downstairs and greeting me at the entrance for another dime. Never underestimate the capabilities of small children.

After two years in Germany, a good American made hamburger was beginning to be missed. Although we were getting use to German culture, there were many things you miss when outside the good old United States. One thing we missed was an American made hamburger.

A B&W Root beer drive-in had opened up in Mannheim, Germany, which was about sixty-five miles from our apartment. We decided one Sunday to drive up for a good old American hamburger. It's not a big deal driving sixty-five miles one way for a hamburger when you have the craving. We decided it was worth the trip.

Our little French car, a 1960 Renault, had finally stopped running with a bad case of too broke to run syndrome. We purchased a brand new Volkswagen Beetle. It was a beauty painted solid red with a white and gray interior. The Volkswagen factory was located only about twelve miles from where we lived.

We paid twelve hundred dollars for the car. Gasoline was twenty cents a gallon when purchased on the base at the Post Exchange.

The Germans were paying around fifty cents a gallon, which was twice the amount Americans were paying for gas in the states.

With snow on the ground in the middle of winter and the outside temperature freezing, the heater in the car was kicking out plenty of warm air and the four of us rode in complete comfort. Being dressed and bundled up in our warmest jackets for the long drive to Mannheim helped too.

The trip back home turned into one those once in a life time experiences. There are no speed limits when driving on the German autobahn highways so I have no idea how fast we were driving, probably around sixty or sixty-five which is fact enough in a Volkswagen Beetle.

All of a sudden, the front windshield shattered! Juliann screamed, "Ice, Ice" and continued crying. She thought it was ice because the windshield had shattered into thousands of tiny pieces. I pulled off the road and when I stopped, the shattered windshield fell to the floorboard and in our laps.

Glass was everywhere. The windshield glass must have been defective because we didn't hear anything strike it. Here we were a good forty miles from home and the temperature in the thirties. Staying awake is easy driving a car with no windshield when it's that cold.

Marian, Juliann and Beth bundled up and crunched down in their seats to keep the cold air off. I did the best I could with my jacket around my head and ears but had one frozen face by the time we arrived home.

It was spring, 1965 and I had to make a big decision soon. My enlistment was coming to an end and I had to decide whether to stay in the Army or get out. My civilian job experience consisted of working in the fields on a farm and part time as a bag boy. It seemed to me money was in short supply on the farm and the salary of a bag boy wouldn't support a wife and two small children. There were no Teletype jobs available in Blackshear or Waycross that I knew of.

My boss was an Army Warrant Officer who had been trying to persuade me to apply for a direct appointment to Warrant Officer. A Warrant Officer is one of those in between grades that most civilians have never heard of until the Viet Nam War. The majority of all helicopter pilots were Warrant Officers. Warrant Officers are supposed to be highly trained and knowledgeable soldiers who can leap tall buildings with a single bound and walk on water. Because of my basketball training, I could leap but not tall buildings and the only person I knew personally that could walk on water was Jesus Christ. Remember Him? He was who I met at church when I was fifteen years old.

Warrant Officers are ranked between the highest enlisted grade and the lowest Commissioned grade. This stuff may be boring but try to pay attention because there may be a test after you read this. There are four warrant officer grades that track closely with commissioned officers for pay purposes. I retired as a Chief Warrant Officer four (CW-4) which would equal a Major as a commissioned officer for pay purposes only. A second lieutenant fresh out of Officer Candidate School outranks a CW4 even those with over twenty years of service. It may same strange but the ranking has served the Army well for many, many years.

Marian and I decided the Army wasn't all that bad and I would apply for a direct appointment to Warrant Officer. The bundles of paperwork were submitted along with some letters of recommendation from my boss and Company Commander telling everyone just how fine a Warrant Officer I would make. They probably figured a little stretching the fine part would be okay since the odds of working with me as a Warrant Officer would be quite slim. It was around four weeks later notification came for me to report to the Warrant Officer Board. Now, the Army likes all type Promotion Boards. For this particular board, it consisted of a Lieutenant Colonel, one Major and one Captain. The routine was to report to the President of the board, take a seat and be prepared to answer all type questions. The routine took around thirty minutes or less.

The board made their recommendations and forwarded the paperwork up to the Department of the Army for approval or disapproval. I received a post card from the Department of Army (DA) in late September saying they received the paperwork and would be in touch later.

It was one of those nice reminders saying they would do the contacting and not bother them with questions. You learn to take things in stride in the Army so I knew to just let the Army take its own sweet time in letting me hear anything on my Warrant Appointment.

Our three years in Germany were coming to an end and my new orders assigned me to Fort Drum, New York with an in-between stop at Fort Gordon Georgia to attend a twenty-six weeks Communications school. We were going home.

Chapter 10

Back To Georgia

Marian, Juliann, Beth and I boarded a charted Boeing 707 for our flight back to America. It was late October 1965. The flight across the Atlantic Ocean took around eight hours. We landed at the International airport at Philadelphia, Pennsylvania. It was almost mid-night and with two small children, we were all exhausted. It was our luck to have to take a cab from the international airport to the domestic airport for a flight to Jacksonville, Florida via Atlanta. Seems that they want let airplanes fly in the south unless they stop in Atlanta first. It was early morning when our flight touched down in Jacksonville. Marian's brother, John Hilton, met us at the terminal and drove us back to Waycross. Arriving home took away a lot of the tired feeling. Three years in a foreign country was a long time to be away from family and friends. Besides, you couldn't find or buy good old American made food in Germany.

Fort Bragg, North Carolina is the home of the eighteenth Airborne Corps. It also was the headquarters of the fairly new army special forces. The Special Forces were implemented during the cold war when President Kennedy directed the Army to establish a quick reaction force. These soldiers along with the soldiers of the Eighteenth Airborne Corps were all airborne qualified parachutists.

For a straight leg, that's what parachutist calls non jumpers like me, the highest thing I'd ever jumped from was the hay barn. Back when I was old enough to know better, I borrowed one of Mama's sheets without her knowledge, fixed it up like a parachute and bailed out of the hayloft. I must have gotten the idea from a comic book or movie show because there was no television to watch.

It's a wonder I didn't break my neck. There are a lot of things I've wanted to do over the years but jumping out of a perfectly good airplane was not on the list. Let em all jump if they wish but this soldier was keeping both feet on the ground. If God had wanted me to jump out of airplanes, my homemade parachute would have opened when I jumped out of the barn.

My first assignment as a warrant officer was Cryptographic Custodian for the signal company I was assigned too. This was no big deal to me in that I was familiar with the duties and had obtained my warrant appointment based on my technical training and experience. It was all the other little special assignments I was appointed to do which were drastically different. The Company Commander appointed me the Voting Officer, Mess Officer, Supply Officer and Training Officer as additional duties. Company Commanders normally appoint commissioned officers to these additional duties so that in case something gets fouled up, he has someone to blame, or that's how it seemed to me at the time.

Being a staff sergeant one day and a warrant officer the next left much room for improvement regarding my qualifications in those other areas. This was a pattern that seemed to be repeated at most of my future assignments. Warrant officers are supposed to be highly trained technicians with a narrow scope of expertise whereby commissioned officers are trained with a broad background structured for command leadership positions. That was the way it was drawn up at the Pentagon anyway.

It became obvious the Army didn't consult mothers when they adapted the warrant officer grade. Mama never did grasp that I was not a corporal, sergeant, lieutenant nor captain and finally gave up asking for a definition.

One day in the middle of June 1966, I received a phone call from the pentagon in Washington, D.C. It was a major from the officer's assignment desk. He began by saying the Army normally gave soldiers three months notice before being assigned overseas but things were heating up in Viet Nam and it was my time to go. He stated I would have two weeks to clear post and two weeks leave time if I requested before shipping out to the First Calvary Division in Viet Nam.

All of my assignments up till then had been at the Army and Corps level. This would be my first assignment at the Division level in the Army. My first tough job was to break the news to Marian. We were living in Government quarters on post so it was only a five-minute drive from my office to our two-bedroom home. She took the news in stride like most dedicated military wives do when confronted with adverse news. We immediately started making housing arrangements for her and the girls while I was away. A three bedroom house was available to rent across the street from John and Ruth Hilton, Marian's brother and sister-in-law. We rented the house for a year for her and the girls while I was in Viet Nam.

The next two weeks flew by. Shortly, we were watching the furniture packers load our household goods for shipment to Waycross. Juliann was four years old and Beth was two. Marian had the task of telling Juliann and Beth I was going away for at least a year. The war in Viet Nam was escalating and more American military personnel were being sent overseas.

It was in late 1965 when the First Cavalry Division was ordered by President Lyndon Johnson to pack up and move the division to Viet Nam from Fort Benning, Georgia. A new concept for fighting a war was going to be tested in battle. It was called airmobile warfare. For over a year, the Army tested an airmobile concept at Fort Benning. It would consist of hundreds of helicopters and equipment that could be airlifted from one battle zone to another. It seemed the perfect method for fighting in jungle terrain.

Viet Nam had its share of jungles, rivers and mountain ridges. Troop strength increased from under one hundred thousand to over three hundred thousand in no time. The fighting forces of the United States would whip the bad North Vietnamese Communists and send them back to where they came. How could a backward country like Viet Nam stand up to the world's strongest military power? Little men in black pajamas didn't stand a chance.

We were to learn a bitter lesson on how not to fight a war in a far away country. You can have the world's best fighting force but if our elected officials can't sell the need for our involvement to the American people, it will fail. History proves it.

The week for me to leave for Viet Nam had arrived. To complicate matters, all commercial airlines were closed due to an Airline Pilots Association strike and the thought of riding a greyhound bus across America to California didn't sound appealing at this point in my life. After checking with the Air Force, I found an Air National Guard flight leaving on Sunday from Savannah to Oakland, California. It was a Sunday afternoon the day I left Waycross for Viet Nam. We attended church services at Central Baptist Sunday morning. We decided to move our church membership back to Central Baptist before I left. Central was Marian's church growing up and also the church we were married in 1959. The drive from Waycross to Hunter Air Force base in Savannah to catch the flight to California was one long, silent trip. Words are hard to come by when choked up with emotion and this was such a time. I loved my wife and daughters more than anything in the world and to leave them for a least a year, with a good chance of never coming home, was a hopeless feeling.

It's amazing how the Lord reaches out and gives us the strength to do those tuff things we have to accomplish sometimes. The lump in the throat was back when we said our goodbye's. A final squeeze and hug for Marian, Juliann and Elizabeth would have to last until my return home at least 365 days later.

Chapter 11

Viet Nam, 1966-1967

It was in the middle of July 1966 when the huge C-141 cleared the runway at Travis Air Force Base, California on the long flight to Viet Nam. With all four engines running at full throttle, the noise inside the aircraft was a constant sound of turning turbines.

The Air Force didn't waste a lot of money on creature comforts for passengers. However, the plane has a remarkable safety record and is considered one of the safest planes to fly. Every soldier onboard was on their way to the 1st Cavalry Division, including me. Our flight to Viet Nam took about eighteen hours. We stopped briefly at Clark Air Force Base in the Philippines to refuel. It was late afternoon on the July 26, 1966 when our flight touched down at Pleiku airfare base, Viet Nam.

This would be the beginning of the first day of our 365 days of duty in Viet Nam. The only way to shorten a one-year tour of duty would be to from a severe wound or be killed and sent home early in a body bag. The temperature was hot and humid. Hot weather is year round in Southeast Asia. During the monsoon seasons, which occur in late fall and winter, the weather may drop to around fifty-five to sixty degrees but not cold weather like we experience in January in South Georgia.

It became apparent from the stifling heat why we were directed to switch from our khaki uniforms to fatigues at our refueling stop in the Philippines. Once we were all off the aircraft, we were split up into group assignments for onward departure to our units.

Those of us assigned to the First Calvary division boarded a Chinook helicopter and departed for An Khe where the division headquarters was located. It was my first glimpse of the countryside.

We flew at around 1500 feet, which gives a good few of the terrain. It was a little spooky to look out the window of the Chinook and see beautiful country and know there were people down there who wanted to kill you.

An Khe is located in the central highlands of Viet Nam. The First Calvary established its main base camp upon their arrival in July 1965, in the jungles adjacent to the city. An Khe itself was a small Vietnamese village located on the main road from Qui Nhon to Pleiku. The complete base area was protected by concertina wire and land mines. Wooden Towers, which stood about thirty feet tall, provided addition protection with two-armed Infantryman in each tower. It appeared to be impregnable but we were to find out it was a long ways from it.

Our helicopter touched down on the landing strip at Division Headquarters, which somebody nicknamed "the golf course". The golf course tag got added because there was nothing there but grass and hundreds of helicopters. Nearby to where the helicopters were parked was a single dirt landing strip. The Army Engineers laid steel planking on the runway to support the weight of aircraft landing and taking off. A corporal was standing by in a jeep to pick me up and take me to my new home, the 13th Signal Battalion. I believe the first words out of his mouth were he only had a few days before his tour of duty ended. The corporal was with the Division in July of 1965 when it first arrived in country. It made my 365 days to serve appears that much longer. I found out later that everyone in country, including me, kept a running calendar, which showed how many days, remained of our tour of duty before going back to the good old United States of America.

The first order of business was to report to the supply tent and turn in our fatigues and boots. We were issued new jungle fatigues and combat boots designed for the jungle warfare. The fatigues were designed to fit lose with pockets everywhere. Our boots were made with a steel shank in the sole and the tops were canvas with eyelets so that when walking in wet terrain, the water could drain out. The steel shank in the sole was supposed to provide some protection from pongee sticks the enemy hid in the trails. The North Vietnamese loved to dip bamboo in a homemade poison and burrow the pongee stick in a path or trail with the hope we would be unfortunate enough to step on the darn thing.

The First Cavalry Division had three brigades and support units consisting of Artillery, Quartermaster, Signal and maintenance units. Two Brigades were kept deployed to search out and make contact with the enemy and one Brigade normally stayed in reserve. My job as

Division Cryptographic Security Officer was to maintain and provide cryptographic equipment and codes for the division. We were using a machine called a KW-7 for teletype security and a machine called a Ky-8 for radio security.

The cryptographic device encrypted everything so anyone without the code was hearing nothing but garble. I was familiar with the KW-7 because we used it in the signal battalion I was stationed with while in Germany. The KY-8 was a different matter. It was completely new and at the time, not being used at all. Our division had quite a few units but they were in a metal shipping container-gathering dust. Somebody in authority cut corners to get the item in the field and it was full of bugs. In other words, it didn't work! Now, I don't know a single thing about how to fix crypto equipment or any other kind of equipment but God saw to it that my senior maintenance sergeant was one of the best in electronics.

Sergeant Mullis was my Maintenance Chief. He had been in country about a month and convinced me his maintenance crew could solve the problem with the KY-8. I knew if he did he would make one Warrant Officer and Battalion Commander rejoice with praise.

A secure voice command and control net would give our division tremendous advantage over the enemy. It was a known fact the North Vietnamese Communist could penetrate our voice radio channels. Listening in on our troop movements by the enemy caused many a soldier his life.

The problem with the KY-8 was caused from one of the printed circuit boards overheating. When the board overheated, the system locked up. The maintenance personnel figured out what area was causing the problem and solved the heat problem with a little backyard maintenance ingenuity. They drilled some holes in the metal case near where the printed circuit board was located. Then, found a small circular fan and plugged it in. Bingo! The heat problem was solved. Installing a KY-8 on the Command and Control Huey helicopters presented another problem. It wasn't practical or feasible to install a fan in the Huey's so the technicians installed a switch between the KY-8's so that when one overheated, the radioman could switch to the other unit. It was the first tactical secure FM net in Viet Nam to my knowledge.

LTC Walt Bodman was the Division Chief Signal Officer and also my boss. He was excited about implementing a secure voice command and control net for the Division. Bodman informed me he had arranged for the Division Staff to be briefed on some new radio equipment our battalion was using and that I could bring them up to date on the KY-8 secure voice equipment. The demonstration would be held at Division Headquarters shortly. This would be my first shot at briefing General Officers on crypto equipment, particularly equipment that so far had failed to operate properly.

I was twenty-nine years old at the time and Bodman seemed concerned about my capabilities to brief in front of high-ranking officers. I had been in country about two weeks and could see my military career crash after our show and tell demonstration. Major General Norton was the Division Commanding General and Brigadier Wright was the Assistant Division Commander. The huge briefing tent was full of other officers in the grade of captain to colonel. My turn to brief arrived.

Although nervous, I thought my presentation was going okay when General Norton stood up and said it was time for a quick break and that I could continue after the break.

The thought crossed my mind that they could use the break because I was putting them to sleep. I was standing up on an ammo case we were using as a briefing platform when General Wright walked up to me and complimented me on my briefing. He then said something to that has stayed with me over the years. He put his arm over my shoulder and told me to relax and take my time. He said the people in the room needed the information and knowledge I was briefing them on. He said they were young soldiers just like me at one time, so relax. I didn't know at the time that I had appeared that nervous but for him to take the time to try and calm my nerves, was important stuff. General Wright later became a four star general and although I wasn't asked for a recommendation, he was one of my favorite generals.

I had been in country for two weeks when a massive mortar and artillery attack was launched against our division. We can move faster than we think possible, when being shot at. It was my first exposure of coming under fire. The problem with a mortar or an artillery barrage is the feeling the rounds are headed straight for your bunker. I had the nerve racking experience that the enemy soldiers were set on taking me out of the fight. They surely had a round zeroed in on my head and it was just a matter of time before it struck. My head gear was my steel pot and I knew it wouldn't stop an AK-47 rifle round must less an incoming artillery shell or mortar round.

The barrage seemed to have lasted an hour but actually only a few minutes. It was my first deep fear of being killed. The thought of dying in a foreign country and not seeing my wife and children again can cause a lot of anxiety and sleepless nights. The division lost three soldiers killed and a few wounded but we found out the next morning it was the helicopters the North Vietnamese were after.

A number of helicopters were destroyed during the attack. It would be the last time the "golf course" launch pad would be used to park helicopters in nice, neat rows. Henceforth, The Division Commander directed that all helicopters be dispersed throughout the Division area. We were still under the false allusion that the North Vietnamese Army was not capable of launching a successful offensive attack.

The first order of business when we moved locations was to dig a bunker adjacent to where we would sleep, when time permits. The bunker actually was a hole in the ground with sandbags stacked around the top of the hole. Every soldier dug his own foxhole. It was the American way in action. All bunkers had to have two layers of sandbags stacked chest high. The division also had a standing policy that all soldiers were required to carry their weapon and wear their steel helmet when outside their tent. Steel pots were designed for safety, and not comfortable like a baseball cap. It was capable of making your head wobble and neck sore, when first worn and headaches were another side affect.

Not only did the First Cavalry have over four hundred helicopters, it must have had a thousand artillery cannon, the most prominent being the 105 howitzer. Throughout the war, Artillery Batteries had pre-selected targets to fire their shells. It was called Harass an Interdiction (H&I) shelling. The objective was to make the enemy feel like his next step would produce artillery rounds right on top of his location. After a few days, the constant sound of artillery shells being fired at the enemy became routine. We are all creatures of our surroundings and the noise factor didn't make an impression until Christmas Day, 1966. The White House negotiated a cease-fire for twenty-four hours so the North Vietnamese and Americans would stop all shooting at each other. I had become so use to the guns going off every few minutes that during the cease-fire, I couldn't go to sleep that night it was so quite.

Every day in Viet Nam was a repeat of the day before. We didn't work an eight to five, five days a week schedule. There were tasks to be completed from the time we woke in the morning until it was possible to sack out at night. Sunday morning was different once a month. For those who wanted to attend church services, we had a Division Chaplain that conducted services when circumstances allowed. It was on a Sunday morning when I was awakened by a tremendous explosion. Shrapnel ripped through our tent and we all dived for cover.

After the blast, suddenly total silence again. If we were under another mortar and artillery barrage, the enemy must have ran out of ammunition after firing one round. The devastating burst was one of our own artillery rounds fired short and hit approximately forty feet from my tent. One soldier was killed and three wounded from the accidental shell blast. Those sorts of tragedies caused by human error didn't happen that frequently, but we did lose soldiers caused from what was referred to as friendly fire. Soldiers in a combat zone, who were on the receiving end of friendly fire, were obviously not consulted by the Army when the name, "friendly fire," was selected.

After a month in Viet Nam, creature comforts of home were beginning to be missed. It was back to the outdoor toilet, no indoor baths or running water and the main meal was Field Ration C and Field Ration D. To explain the difference between the two rations, C rations were in small cans and D rations were in large cans. I'm sure the Army spent a fortune developing numerous ways to keep food from spoiling and trying their best to offer balanced meals to us soldiers, but believe me, C rations are a long way from home cooking.

When we were at base camp, the meal was D rations, which is a step above a C ration. Matter of fact, some of the meals, even though all of them came from a can, was not that bad. Come to think of it, they were not so good though. C rations were issued to soldiers in the field and were eaten cold for the most part. We were issued thermal tablets which could be dropped into a empty can and provide enough heat to warm the meal once the thermal tablets caught fire and burned a long burning low flame.

A ration box was issued for about ten soldiers and consisted of gum, candy, cigarettes, and a couple of toothbrush's, toothpaste, razor blades and a few other odds and end for our use. The candy was tootsie rolls and M&M's. I must have thought there was going to a razor blade shortage in America because I saved my extra blades and had enough when I rotated to the states to start my on store. The odds and ends were writing tablets, ballpoint pens and Kool-Aid packets. One of my maintenance men was complaining one day about the fact a Kool-Aid packet was made for a quart of juice and we used our canteen cups to mix and drink. He said they should make a cup size packet. I told him to complain to the Kool-Aid folks so he did. He wrote them a letter using the paper lid from a C ration box for paper.

Writing tablets were available but he wanted to put special emphasis on his request and wrote something to the effect that the paper he was using to write on was all that was available deep in the jungle of Viet Nam. It was about two months later when he received a very nice letter from Kool-Aid thanking him for his letter and the fact he was drinking their product. They went on to say that unfortunately there was no market for that size packet in the United States. To show their appreciation for his effort of writing them, they sent him two cases of cool-Aid. We never ran out of the stuff during my year in Viet Nam. To the best of my knowledge, I haven't drunk any more Kool-Aid sense 1967

Chapter 12

Dear John Letter

Approximately three months had passed when another maintenance technician was assigned to my unit. He had been in country less than a month when mail from home caught up with him. It took from one to two weeks for mail to go from South Georgia to Viet Nam. One of the few nice things about mailing a letter was we didn't have to buy stamps. All we had to do was write on the envelope the word "free". It might take another two weeks before the Army got it sorted out and sent to the right spot.

When he opened the letter from his mother and began reading, she made the serious mistake of writing her son that his wife was having an affair. His immediate reaction to me was that he had to go home on emergency leave to try and save his marriage. I didn't say anything to him but the thought did cross my mind that his wife sure didn't spin her wheels finding a new soul mate, because he had only been in Vietnam a short period of time.

The Army has procedures established to cover emergency situations when the circumstances are serious enough. The death of a parent, brother or sister, wife or child is examples that would be considered.

Going home because your wife was having an affair was not considered urgent or serious according to the Army guidelines so his request to go home and try and save his marriage was disapproved. Unfortunately, the turndown was too much for him to handle. He went berserk. It was the first time I've ever witnessed a person going completely out of control. He was actually foaming at the mouth. We called the medics who transported him to a field hospital and subsequently, to a military hospital in Japan for treatment. He was never sent back to our unit and I assume, eventually evacuated home under a medical discharge.

Two months had passed when the phone rang one afternoon. It was the Battalion Operations Officer calling to tell me a full colonel from Saigon was at his office and would be coming over to inspect our Cryptographic facility. Cryptographic equipment and operational codes require stringent security protection to insure everything is accounted for and only authorized personnel with the proper security clearance have access.

The phone call caught me off guard but I thought that it probably was just another way of insuring everything was being done properly. I escorted the colonel into our secure facility where he did a one hundred percent inventory on all our equipment and codes. It took little over two hours but he found everything okay and departed.

After the colonel's departure, the Operations Officer called me to his office and showed me the real reason for the inspection. My Maintenance Technician who had the nervous breakdown wrote his Congressman that I was selling classified equipment and codes to the enemy. The Congressman forwarded the letter to the department of the Army where it had wound its way through the chain of command to the Inspector General's Office in Saigon. The colonel was sent to check out the letter and if found true, probably send me straight to prison if I was lucky or straight to a firing squad for spying. He did make the allegation in the letter but it kind of gave you a clue that maybe the letter writer wasn't all there because most of the letter was unintelligible.

The Army probably has a rule that says every complaint must be checked out. As it turned out, the surprise inspection worked in my favor. It seems every time I step in a deep hole, along comes my special angel to dig me out. About two weeks later, it was the Operations Officer calling again informing me to standby for a surprise inspection by the Assistant Commanding General. General Wright had rotated back to the states and Brigadier General Blanchard was his replacement. My first thought was another letter written by the unfortunate Maintenance Technician had bounced down the chain of command again. Anyway, General Blanchard showed up and I started escorting him through the facility. He spent about a two minutes looking around and then headed for the exit door. Colonel Bodman was at the door and turned to the General and said didn't the General have something for me.

The inspection was a sham so the General could pin a Commendation Medal on me for the good inspector general's report.

Talk about turning a devastating event from an unfortunate situation to an Atta-boy for me could only be accomplished by my special angel.

After being in Viet Nam six months, I switched jobs with the Warrant Officer who handled the Division Communications Center. This relieved me from being responsible for all the super secret stuff but it meant my next six months would be in the boondocks full time. My admiration for our young men who served in the Infantry increased tenfold during my year in Viet Nam. It is one thing to withstand an occasional mortar or artillery attack but it is something else when everyday is spent trying to survive a firefight with the enemy. Although we were all in a combat zone, Support troops are in a more secure perimeter than our front line Infantrymen. Our Division forward element moved frequently.

Our airmobile capability provided the division a lot of flexibility to fight the North Vietnamese Communist. Division Forward was set up at a landing zone (LZ) called LZ Hammond. LZ Hammond was located a couple of miles from the coastline, which was the South China Sea. First Cavalry Division Forward was positioned at this location. We could relocate a complete brigade with necessary support attachments in about two days. The Army Engineers did a good job of clearing the underbrush so our equipment and tents could be set up.

All equipment to include the Division Forward headquarters was protected by a parameter secured by the Infantry; along with strands of concertina wire interlaced with claymore mines. Sandbags and railroad ties were used for reinforcement. The Engineers were good at their job. They made moving small mountains with their equipment seem easy. Every piece of communications gear in the division was configured so it could be moved by helicopter. The largest piece of equipment was mounted on jeep trailers. A Chinook helicopter would come in and hover in place while a sling was dropped to hook up the equipment. Once secured properly, it was airlifted to its new location. This gave us tremendous flexibility in fighting the Vietnamese Communist (VC) and North Vietnamese.

The war in Viet Nam was unique in that there were no front lines. For the most part, the VC controlled the countryside except where our forces were located and some surrounding nearby terrain. We were fortunate in our Division in that we controlled the air and used helicopters to move from place to place.

My new home was a two-man tent. A First Lieutenant from Texas named Arial was my tent mate. Naturally, with a name like Arial, we nicknamed him TV. TV was a country boy like me. We were good friends during our tour of duty. He was a Radio Officer responsible for insuring the voice and Teletype circuits were installed and operational. Monsoon season was going full blast in January 1967. The next six months creped by. Although our job each day was to insure that the Divisions telecommunications were received, delivered and sent out, we were in the center of a combat zone.

The First Cavalry had a quick reaction squadron broken down into two teams. One team was called the red team and the other the blue team. Their mission was for one team to be airlifted into a known or suspected enemy position and draw fire from the enemy so that the other team plus coordinated reinforcements could be brought to bear to destroy the enemy.

Every time I had the slightest hint of feeling sorry for myself I thought of those brave men in the quick reaction Squadron. On one particular day, the squadron made contact and was in a vicious firefight less than a mile from our location. It was like watching a movie to see the Air Force Phantom jets roar in and drop their bombs from about 500 feet elevation. All I could see was the blast followed by the sound of the explosion. It wasn't a movie. Soldiers were being killed and wounded.

Our Infantrymen had called for air strikes almost on their own position. The dark side of human nature tended to come out for some who were in the war. It is one thing to have to defend yourself and fight for what you believe in your heart is the right thing to do in combat. It is unthinkable to enjoy killing another human no matter what the circumstances. We had those amongst us who boasted that they enjoyed killing. One of my young men committed a callous and unforgettable act that shook me and caused me to wonder what makes people tick. The Army loves to have soldiers pull different type details, which in most cases were day-to-day sanitation jobs. Like being tasked to haul off garbage to the trash dump built nearby by the Engineers. Two men were tasked each day to haul off a jeep trailer load of trash and garbage. The dump was on the other side of the little village called Bong Son. It was around eleven o'clock one morning when two MP's showed up and wanted to know if a certain corporal was in my unit. They reported that when the trash detail were driving through Bong Son, the one not driving unclipped a grenade and tossed it in a Vietnamese hut. Now, we were there to protect and free the South Vietnamese from the communist, not go around killing the civilians.

The young man was only eighteen years old. He was one of my best soldiers as for as doing his job and not causing trouble. He joined the Army when he was seventeen and had been in Viet Nam about the same length of time as me. When interrogated by the police, he said that it just came over him that all Vietnamese were the enemy and he was only doing his duty. Fortunately, nobody was killed. There were two people in the hut who were severely wounded but survived. The young soldier was court-marshaled and given prison time for his action. I knew of two other men who volunteered to remain in Viet Nam for another year because as they said, they thought war was fun.

Every day was rain and more rain. Nothing we had could be kept dry. Raining every day for weeks, tuned the ground into a muddy quagmire. To make matters worse, the strong winds caused some large rips in our tent one night and everything got soaked. Trying to find dry clothing became a constant problem during the monsoon season.

We all slept under mosquito netting because of the risk of catching malaria. Mosquitoes love wet, damp areas to breed and they felt right at home in Vietnam. The risk of catching malaria was a daily risk in the central highlands of Vietnam. Every day we were supposed to swallow a pill big enough to choke a horse to cut down on the risk of malaria. Surprisingly, I knew of some that deliberately failed to take their pill hoping they would come down with malaria so they could be sent home via medical evacuation. I wanted to leave but not that way.

The next morning, we were off looking for a new tent. Luckily, our Supply Officer was another Warrant Officer, so we were issued a brand new tent to replace the damaged one. The Army is just like the civilian world. It's not what you know but whom you know.

It was the spring of 1967 when we jumped from LZ Hammond to a new landing zone located near the village of Bong Song located on the coast. My tour was getting shorter by the day. When word came to relocate to a new site, it meant moving our radio relay and telecommunications equipment for the new area. We obtained enough communications equipment to leave our facility at LZ Hammond intact until we established our communication Link at the new site. It was late evening when a handful of advance party moved out for our new location.

We were dropped off via helicopter at our new site, which was adjacent to a Special Forces Camp. Now, the Special Forces were in a well-established camp with plenty of concertina wire and land mines to provide some protection. Land mines used were the type called a Claymore mine, which fired off a tremendous charge when activated. Claymores were about the size of a shoebox with a slight curve in the middle. You set them up so that the curved part of the mine was pointed toward the area you wanted the charge or explosion to go.

Our Vietnamese adversaries were good at penetrating our perimeters and turning the mine where it went off in our direction instead of theirs. We were on the outside of the perimeter without any protection other than ourselves. Most soldiers were issued the M-16 rifle. It was fairly new at the time and had replaced the Armies M-14, which was a much larger, and heaver weapon. The M-16 was light and could fire at semi-automatic or automatic.

My issued weapon was an Army 45 caliber pistol. They probably figured I might hurt myself with the M-16. There were about ten of us in the advance party to set up the equipment and establish communications back to Division Headquarters. It was around seventy-two hours before the rest of the advance forces in the division joined us. None of us slept or took a bath for the next seventy-two hour period. You can stay awake real easy with the right type motivation.

After being awake continuously for about eighteen hours, your body slows down and everything seems to be going in slow motion. Even your speech is affected. Ask a question to someone and about a minute later, you might get an answer. Thankfully, we were not required to do any heavy thinking other than how to stay alive and survive.

Chapter 13

Going Home

My tour of duty was almost up. Orders reassigning me back to Fort Gordon arrived with a departure date of July 23, 1967. I had three weeks left. Time slowed to a crawl. It probably was the longest three weeks of my life. I was relieved of my duties three days before my departure and caught a Huey Helicopter back to Division Main at An Khe. Normally, flying in a helicopter with both doors open just above tree top level didn't bother me. It wasn't uncommon to have a twenty-year-old Warrant Officer flying the chopper and some of them loved to fly above the treetops and on occasion, clip the tops of a few trees with the landing struts.

Flying low also lessoned the risk of being a target for the enemy. It became our primary means of transportation and the risks were taken at face value without a lot of concern. We tend to think of ourselves as being invisible when we're in our twenties and taking chances is part of growing up I guess. Now that I was beginning the first leg of my checking out of Viet Nam, worry slowly started creeping into my thoughts and feelings.

I prayed a silent prayer to Jesus to see me and the chopper crew safely back to An Khe. My prayer was answered and we arrived back without incident. A new Battalion Commander took command of the 13th Signal Battalion prior to my departure. In his first week as commander, he fired three lieutenants because he wasn't satisfied with their performance of duty. My tent mate was about to have a stroke. Ariel was trying to avoid the Lieutenant Colonel at all costs. He still had two months to go on his tour and was trying his best to leave country with a good performance report.

I was relieved of all my duties when my replacement arrived, so it was just a wait until my flight home was scheduled. I asked the new commander a few days before I left why he was so rough on lieutenants. He said the Army was letting too many bad lieutenants serve and it was his responsibility to weed them out. He wanted to know if I would consider extending my tour of duty. My reply was no way and wondered to myself if the word stupid appeared anywhere on my forehead.

On departure day, I crawled up on the floor bed of a C-130 at An Khe for departure to Pleiku for subsequent flight on a C-141 back to America. All seats were missing. We sat on the floor bed with our knees drawn up as close together as possible. I didn't give it a second thought because we were headed home but I'm sure the Air Force has rules against flying passengers bunched up on the floor of their aircraft, with no seatbelts.

Once we landed at Pleiku, we turned in our jungle fatigues, boots and were searched for contraband. Every soldier who served in Viet Nam probably accumulated some souvenirs to take home. I was no exception. Our division captured a lot of weapons; flags and other artifacts used by the North Vietnamese. Most of the stuff I had was harmless. I had a few rounds of enemy ammo, a captured North Vietnamese flag and some other junk. Nobody got out with a souvenir but at that time, I could care less. I didn't need a reminder to take home to remember the place. Waycross, here I come.

The C-141 looked the same, as the one I arrived in except this one appeared to have a majestic glow with a close resemblance of a beautiful angel. It wouldn't have bothered me the least to glance out the aircraft window and see the wings flapping like a dove. The aircraft was just as noisy as the other one but the noise this time had a pleasant and restful sound. I've never been afraid of flying but the thought did cross my mind that crashing on my way home would mess up one enjoyable homecoming with my wife and children.

It seemed like a dream to finally be out of Viet Nam. No more sleeping bags with mosquito netting and back to the world of indoor toilets, running water and fresh food. I would miss the constant sound of artillery rounds going off but figured I could survive the adjustment. Halleluiah! Free at last, free at last.

Jesus teaches in his word that those of us who believe in him should live in liberty and not in fear. It is a constant struggle for Christians like me to avoid trying to live by our own wits and turn our everyday life over to God to guide and direct our every action. When I was a babe in Christ, so to speak, I thought maybe God was too busy for me to bother him with the little things and just confront him with the big whoppers. I know better today.

My special angel wouldn't have had to work so hard lifting me out of holes and maybe could take early angel retirement.

The C-141 touched down at Travis Air Force Base in California. The thought crossed my mind to kiss the pavement but I didn't. It was beginning to feel like a dream. Just eighteen hours ago I was living in a war zone and now it was normal again. Everybody spoke English, even the small children. The smell in the air was so refreshing! What a relief. The odor of latrines was gone. No longer did I have to smell the burning residue of latrines soaked with gasoline and set afire and burned. This process filled the air with a putrid smell that's hard to forget, even now.

We were bussed by the Air Force to the Civilian Air terminal to catch our flight for home. It was around eleven p.m. when I dialed Marian to tell her my flight number and time of arrival in Jacksonville, Florida.

My departure was on a Delta Airlines flight to Atlanta where I would switch to Eastern Airlines. It was early in the morning when the Eastern aircraft departed Atlanta for the hour flight to Jacksonville. The aircraft was a Boeing 707, which was capable of hauling over two hundred passengers. Nobody asked me had I been to Vietnam. There were no welcome home signs. "Thank you for your service to our country," was not part of the American vocabulary during the Vietnam War. Thankfully, there were no protests either.

There were less than twenty passengers on the flight to Jacksonville. The flight took about one hour. By the time the 707 reaches cruising altitude, it's time to start making its landing decent. Anxiety began to set in. Was it really a dream or would I be seeing my family in a few minutes? If it was a dream, I didn't want to wake up. Marian, Juliann and Beth were at the terminal waiting. Thank you, Lord, for taking care of my family and bringing me back to America safe and hopefully, sound.

One of the smartest decisions Marian made was to rent a beach cottage at Fernandina Beach my first week back in the states. The next morning all four of us got up early and loaded the little red Volkswagen and headed down US one highway toward Fernandina Beach. It was the first time I'd driven a vehicle in a year.

We had been on the road about ten minutes when I pulled over and asked Marian to drive. My mind was switching back and forth between being home and being back in Viet Nam. I broke out in a cold sweat. What's going on? What's happening to me? Am I still dreaming? Panic set in and I didn't trust my on reactions to driving feeling like I did.

After we arrived at our cottage, my feeling of panic and fear settled down. Later, I was to learn it was a normal reaction I experienced for soldiers returning from the war. What was happening was the almost instant changing from one environment to another without letting our feelings and emotions adjust.

All six of our senses are challenged from one extreme to the other. I felt secure and not afraid. I saw beautiful scenery without the fear of approaching men in black pajama's trying to kill me. I smelled the air without a hint of gunpowder. I could feel and touch my wife and children and sleep at night not worrying about their safety. I could hear the wind blowing without the sound of helicopter rotor blades chopping through the air. I could eat a good home cooked meal and taste the freshness. It didn't take me long to readjust to being back in a safe environment and adjusting to a normal routine just like most normal civilians. Unfortunately, there were many who returned that didn't fare so well. Doctors and those folks who study human emotions called what we experienced Post Traumatic Syndrome or something similar.

Our vacation at the beach was spent reacquainting us to each other. Juliann and Beth were a year older and Daddy was somebody that their Mama talked to them about but who they had almost forgotten. It would take some time before the girls felt comfortable enough to ask Daddy for things instead of just Mama. The next week was spent traveling up to Augusta, Georgia once again to look for a house to rent. There were very little military housing available at Fort Gordon in 1967 so we didn't bother to see if anything was available. Besides, we wanted to get back into a community where our girls could settle down and enjoy some time with both mama and daddy.

The first of August 1967 was another hot, humid day in Augusta. It gets hot in South Georgia but Augusta takes the cake on truly hot weather. My days working in the hot tobacco fields of South Georgia gave me a head start adjusting to the stifling heat of Viet Nam and the hot weather of Augusta. This would be our third move back to Augusta after eight years of marriage.

It was beginning to feel like where we belonged. New homes and sub divisions were springing up all over the Augusta area. We spent a lot of evenings riding around looking at new homes and dreaming of one we could afford. Why, it's the American dream to be a new homeowner and we were no different. A new sub-division was expanding rapidly nearby to where we were renting our house. After much soul searching, we decided to make the plunge. Besides, I could finance it through the VA, which helped on the down payment. That was the big pitch, one hundred dollars down with a VA loan on a brand new three bedroom, two-bath brick home we decided to have built.

The time came shortly for us to meet the builder at the bank to sign the paperwork. Our new home was being financed for thirty years at six percent interest. The cost was $15,750.00. Our monthly payment to include taxes and insurance was $112.00 a month. At the time, it felt like we would we in debt for the rest of our lives. The good news was it would be our home along with the bank.

The war was continuing to heat up and more and more military equipment and personnel were being sent to Viet Nam. Every male between the age of eighteen and twenty-five was eligible for the draft and ripe for call to active duty. The only exception was men who could not pass a physical and college students with a valid deferment.

President Johnson made the decision not to call up the reserves which meant all eligible men stood a good chance of going to Viet Nam. Opposition to the War effort was also starting to attract more and more Americans. College students in some of our finest colleges held massive demonstrations protesting our government's action. It didn't make sense to me. College students whose parents had the financial resources to send them to school and avoid the draft were protesting against those of us who served proudly.

The flags of our enemy were waved proudly at demonstrators while the American flag was flown upside down and in more extreme cases, burned in front of cheering crowds. Patriotism was not at the front of the line for a lot of Americans. Soldiers returning from the war were confronted by mobs screaming "baby killers, baby killers". Our vocabulary along with our values seemed to be upside down. Grass wasn't referring to the green farm fields but marijuana joints smoked like a cigarette. Getting high didn't mean going up in an airplane or drinking a few beers. Buying coke wasn't referring to a cool refreshing coca cola but instead meant a sniff of cocaine. Avoiding the draft and moving to Canada didn't faze a lot of people. We even had some so-called distinguished Americans travel to Russia and North Vietnam and offered encouragement to our enemy while American soldiers died in the rice patties and jungles of Viet Nam. Military men brave enough to wear their uniforms were booed, jeered and accused of all kinds of unmentionable atrocities.

Protesting demonstrators, many dressed to disgrace the American flag and a few not dressed at all, were cheered as heroes. All of a sudden, what was right was now wrong and what was wrong was now right. America was living in a nightmare as far as I was concerned.

Our new home was completed in December 1967. There is a special feeling of accomplishment in owning a home, especially the first one. It's probably at the top of the list for young married couples. I was now an old man at age thirty but felt ten feet tall knowing we had a home we could call our own. Besides, driving a 1964 red Volkswagen Beetle wasn't all that bad for a brand new homeowner. Landscaping was not of our home purchasing package so there were plenty of things that required action after we moved in. Buying and planting shrubs and getting the yard presentable were a daily chore after coming home from work. While working daily in the yard to establish nice green grass and scrubs, we found out that the contractors buried loads of left over building material in the ground instead of hauling it to the dump. Probably saved them some money but left a big, ugly mess when we kept digging the junk up trying to establish our yard.

Most men that I know don't like to hang pictures, curtains or curtain rods and I am no exception. It's has to be done though, but it has always puzzled me how you can hang a picture in a brand new wall without hammering a few nail holes someplace. I can here Marian saying, "Thomas, be careful and don't drive in too many nail holes in the new walls". For men like me who tend to get the first nail hole and sometimes the second nail hole in the wrong spot, always have a tube of white toothpaste handy. A little dab will do wonders hiding unwanted nail holes in the wall.

Juliann was now in the first grade. The big yellow school bus stopped about seventy-five feet from our front door for her to board. This would be Juliann's second school. She ultimately attended at least six more before graduating from Ware County School in 1978. Moving as much as we did over a twenty-three year period is about normal for a career military family. At first, we thought the frequent moving would become a handicap for our children. Actually, it helped in their education. Both of them were forced to learn to make new friends quickly and also to learn to say goodbye faster than they wanted.

Chapter 14

Assignment White House Communications Agency

It was a typical spring day in April 1968, when I received a telegram from the Defense Communications Agency in Arlington, Virginia. The telegram directed me to come to their headquarters for consultations. I wasn't sure what it meant but knew that in the military, you don't sit back and say, "I don't think I want to do that". I knew Arlington, Virginia was near the Pentagon and wondered if it could have something to do with an assignment to the pentagon. Drawing an assignment to the Washington, DC area wasn't at the top of most soldiers' wish list. It was an extremely high cost of living area and nobody volunteered that I knew of.

The telegram stated for me to report to the Administrative Building at eight o'clock in the morning and to be dressed in my class "A" uniform. In 1968, my weight was around one hundred and sixty pounds and my hair was cut short in a crew cut. It was the style then and it seemed military personnel tried to see who could have their hair cut the shortest. Some even wore the shaved look. My flying saucer headgear was a perfect fit.

Ten years later I dug my uniform out of mothballs, for my retirement ceremony and discovered my headgear wouldn't fit. "Marian, my head has gotten bigger these last few years. I got the big head. My headgear want fit." I hollered. "You silly man, you wore a crew cut when you bought hat. Go have your head shaved and it will still fit", she said.

My trip to the Pentagon in 1963 riding the train was enjoyable plus convenient so I decided to take the train again. Leaving Augusta, Georgia in the afternoon and riding all night in a Pullman was an enjoyable way to travel. Beside, you can see things out the window of a train even at night. The train pulled into Union Station in Washington, D.C. around 0700 hours. That's 7 am for the non-military.

It took about ten minutes for the cab driver to drive the short distance to the Defense Communications Agency (DCA) located in Arlington, Virginia. A young man dressed in a neat suit was waiting to take me for my interview at the White House Communications Agency

Administrative building was located in the Georgetown section of D.C.

My first appointment was with the commander of the headquarters unit. The Army colonel was dressed in a suit instead of his military uniform. At the time, it seemed strange to be talking with military people who were on duty but not in their uniform. After around twenty minutes, my first interview was completed and I proceeded to be interviewed by other department heads.

My last appointment was with the Agency Commander. The interview with Colonel Albright was short and to the point. He stated his staff was saying good things about me but if I wanted to be considered, I had to phone my wife before I decided and get her opinion and okay. This was the first time any military commander had asked me to consult with my wife before making a decision regarding an assignment. During the many interviews, I was told that a lot of traveling would entail with the assignment and my first position would be as a Duty Officer, which is shift work.

Marian and I decided living in the Washington, D.C. area and working shift work with a lot of traveling thrown in was better than me going back to Viet Nam for another twelve months. Besides, the North Vietnamese were using real bullets and I still had lots of things to accomplish before my time on earth expired.

Although I already held a top-secret security clearance, the Agency required all potential assignees undergo another background check plus agree to take a polygraph examination. Len Stephens was the Agency Security Officer. Len was an Army Warrant Officer who was originally from South Carolina. He had developed a reputation for being an outstanding Communication Trip Officer when traveling with the president. He briefed me on what security requirements were necessary for the job. His staff started filling out the paperwork to run another background investigation on me. They also set up an appointment for my polygraph examination. It would be my first and last lie detector test. Gosh, the government could now find out about all the mean and dirty things I had done. Actually, the test wasn't all that terrible.

The administrative fellow, who hooked me up to the machine, gave me a run down on the type questions asked. He first said he would ask a series of questions, which the correct response should be yes, but for me to answer no. He could monitor my responses to see what kind of impact it made with the little gages jittering around on the graph paper. He didn't say it but probably wanted to see if I was a good liar. After a few questions and some adjustments to the polygraph dials, he proceeded with the examination.

It took about ten to fifteen minutes to complete the polygraph test. Later, he told me I did fine and passed as for as he was concerned. It just goes to show that being raised on a farm has some hidden advantages. There wasn't much you could do to get in trouble living on a farm in South Georgia.

My background investigation by the FBI would be initiated and all I had to do was go back to Fort Gordon and wait on the results. I was assured I would be notified if I passed the background or failed and that they wouldn't just send the cops to arrest me if anything really bad popped up on the background check. It was the middle of June when I received a telephone call and told my background investigation was complete and orders assigning me to the Agency would be sent shortly. My assignment with the White House Communications Agency was about to begin.

Chapter 15

Lyndon Baines Johnson

Lyndon Johnson was in his last six months as President of the United States. America was in a state of turmoil. In Washington, D.C., rioters and demonstrators filled the streets after Dr. Martin Luther King was assassinated. The civil disobedience plus all the demonstrators protesting the war raging in Viet Nam was taking its toll on the President.

He made his famous announcement back in March that he would not run for reelection. He told the nation in a television broadcast, "I shall not seek, and I will not accept, the nomination of my party for another term as your President". He stated his motivation not to run was to help heal the wounds dividing America caused by the war raging in Viet Nam.

I remember during my interview for the job everyone was speaking of the upcoming election and how much extra work Presidential elections caused. The thought probably crossed my mind since President Johnson was not running for reelection; the job should be routine. It didn't take long after reporting for duty to see how wrong I was.

The war in Viet Nam continued to escalate and anti war demonstrators drew larger crowds with their get of Viet Nam rallies. Demonstrators were camping on the grounds at the Washington Monument and on the mall when I drove into D.C. my first day of duty. Agency personnel were issued parking passes, which allowed us to park on the ellipse adjacent to the White House. Even with a parking pass, it was still hard to find a vacant spot to park. Tourist loved to fill up the parking spots and probably figured the D.C. police wouldn't spend a lot of time tacking them down in whatever state they were from.

The hippie movement was gaining momentum. Most of the demonstrators were dressed in typical hippie attire with long stringy hair. It was hard to tell the boys from the girls because wearing of beads was also in fashion for the counter-culture crowd. My thoughts back then was if they don't mess with me I won't mess with them. Although we didn't wear our military uniforms while on duty at the White House, I was proud to be an Army Warrant Officer.

It didn't make sense to me to be demonstrating against our government. America was a nation where people by the thousands try to inter every day. We didn't have folks fighting to get out. For the most part, I thought it was just a bunch of rich college kids who were to chicken to be drafted and serve their country when called. Popping acid, pills, sniffing cocaine and smoking grass were also part of the anti-war movement.

It seemed that the children of our most prosperous and well off families were driven to drown their happiness with something that blew their minds. It was a mix I never have figured out.

My first few days as a Duty Officer was primarily spent getting familiar with the physical layout of communication facilities maintained and operated by WHCA plus the layout of the White

House and adjoining Executive Office Building (EOB). The White House Signal switchboard along with the Teletype facilities feeding messages to the Situation Room was located in the basement of the White House. The Duty Officer office was also in the basement.

When asked where we worked, we could say the White House. It sounded better than telling folks we worked in the basement. There were two switchboards, which served the White House. The administrative switchboard was operated and maintained by the General Service Administration. It's the switchboard reached when calling the White House number listed in the phone book. The switchboard operated by WHCA was called the Signal Board and used to connect all government agencies to the White House.

The switchboard was a five position manually operated switching center manned by young men and women who handled the thousands of calls from the White House Staff, Secret Service and other governmental departments twenty-four hours every day. They performed their duties with remarkable efficiency and ability to find people all over the world. This was back when people efficiency played a major part of providing the best service available, to the President, his family and staff.

Although there were newer systems available, the phones in the White House and staff, were provided what was called off hook service. The Chief Of Staff to the President and other key personnel could pick up the phone and a Signal operator would answer and place the call. George Kranich, who was the enlisted Non Commissioned Officer (NCO) in charge of the switchboard section, developed and implemented a remarkable training school used to teach operators how to be the best of the best. George was assigned to WHCA during the Kennedy Administration. He went on to spend over twenty years assigned to WHCA. Former Presidents and others who had access to the Signal Switchboard, have written about their uncanny ability to track down people no matter were located.

There were also some unpleasant situations the operators had to endure. President Johnson was famous for his "hands on" approach in being President and didn't mince words when he felt it was necessary to make his point, which was about all the time. Johnson didn't deal through his staff but went straight to the source when he wanted something accomplished.

Normally, the Signal Operator with the most experience was assigned to monitor and handle calls for the residence and Oval Office. On this particular call, the operator was in the middle of completing a call for Secretary Of Defense McNamara when the red light over the President's extension, lit up. The operator completed the connection for Mr. McNamara before answering the President's line, which was probably less than two seconds. When he plugged into the jack to answer the call, President Johnson asked what took him so long and was he taking a nap. Now, the operator made a fatal blunder and responded to the President that he was completing a call for Mr. McNamara when his line buzzed. This excuse didn't go over well and Mr. Johnson informed the operator Mr. McNamara worked for him and when his line lit up; everything else took a back seat. He also said he just might have him shipped to a military base so far away that sunlight would have to be piped in. I'm sure he was just kidding but we never knew when dealing with President Johnson.

When a foreign Head of State visits the White House, the arrival ceremony is usually held on the South Portico of the White House. My first time seeing President Johnson occurred while on the South Lawn. The Audio Visual Technicians were busy installing the sound system for a state visit. Major Ed Nelson, who was in charge of the Audio Visual Branch, had taken me out with him to view the communication setup for a Chief of State visit. It was my second day on duty. His technicians were busy setting up a Public Address (PA) system for the ceremony and all the other equipment necessary at an event where the President would be speaking. The podium and two tape recorders were hooked up along with an audio feed for the National News media.

To prevent the media from hanging microphones all over the podium, the Agency used an audio feed box, which had multiple plugs for the media to plug into to pick up a direct audio feed from the podium.

Ed Nelson and I were standing around observing the installation of the sound equipment when President Johnson walked out on the south lawn and motioned for Ed to come over. He had to be pointing to Ed because there was no way under the sun he knew who I was.

We both walked up to him and he told Major Nelson he wanted him to find out who installed the last sound system for a South Lawn ceremony because he wanted him to set it up just like it was done by the other fellow. He said it was the best sound system he had ever heard and he wanted it done exactly the same way. "Yes sir, Mr. President. It will be done." Major Nelson replied. He contacted his office to find out who was in charge of installing the last sound system.

The audio technician was located and he told Maj Nelson that the only thing was done differently than normal procedures was to place one of the long, narrow speakers up under the speaker's platform pointing directly up under the raised platform where the president would be speaking from.

When the President began his speech, his remarks were being blasted up to him from the speaker below the platform and naturally he was hearing everything loud and clear. People who speak or sing love to hear their own voice. That's why there is sound monitors positioned on stage when they perform. I might be an exception since I was born without any singing or speaking talent. Actually, if for some reason I start humming while taking a shower, it makes me nauseous.

The Officers and Warrant Officers had the best job of anyone in the Agency. All we had to do was make sure the enlisted technicians knew the when, where and what the mission was and to make sure adequate resources and manpower were available. It didn't hurt to know how to interact with the White House Staff, U. S. Secret Service Agents and the White House Press Office. It was a delight to be serving with men and women who were selected to serve in the Agency and performed their jobs brilliantly. The Officers and Warrant Officers who failed in the majority of cases were those who tried to micro manage their personnel.

Everybody knew President Johnson was impatient when dealing with subordinates, which included almost everyone except maybe his immediate family. One of the requirements of the Duty Officer was to make sure all communication requests from the President, Secret Service and Staff were handled quickly and efficiently after normal business hours. A communication technician from each department, were required to be on standby for emergency situations. The Duty Officer could reach technicians who were on standby duty by phone at all times. They had to be able to be at the White House complex in less than an hour when notified.

It was around nine p.m. one weekend when I received a phone call from the Ushers office stating the President couldn't get his portable tape recorder working so he wanted someone immediately to come up and get it fixed. It dawned on me that one hour was longer than Mr. Johnson would probably wait and action of some sort was needed immediately. The Maintenance Chief on duty in the Cryptographic Equipment Section was a Navy Chief Petty Officer named Dan Schottlekotte. I buzzed his office and asked him to come to the office as quickly as possible. When Dan entered the office, his arm was in a sling. He had broken a bone in his right arm. I told Dan the President required help with his tape recorder and for him to go up to the residence and check it out until the standby radio technician arrived. I told him he could take the tape recorder and attempt to be working on it to stall for some precious time.

Dan said he didn't know anything about fixing tape machines and besides; his arm was in a sling. Dan was a very bright technician and like most of us didn't seek out direct contact with the President if at all possible. I told Dan somebody had to go up to the residence quick because the President wouldn't wait long, and I figured it better he than me. At least he was trained in maintenance because I couldn't repair a piece of equipment if my life depended on it. In less than five minutes, Dan was back in my office. He had a big grin on his face when I asked him what was he doing back down so quickly. "I fixed the tape recorder, "Dan Said. "The President had installed the batteries in backward." It goes to show even Presidents needs help with the little things in life sometime.

Videotape machines for home use were not available in 1968. A company called Ampex invented videotaping so the capability was available for commercial use. There were two Ampex taping machines installed for use in the White House. The two machines filled up a small room in the executive office building (EOB) located inside the white house complex across from the West Wing. Videotape was two inches thick on large reels. It was standard procedure for all newscasts and Presidential speeches broadcast via television to be recorded.

Gunsmoke with Matt Dillon and Kitty was also recorded weekly as standard practice. Lady Bird Johnson loved the program and wanted to make sure she didn't miss a single episode. A closed circuit video feed was installed throughout the White House and EOB for rebroadcast of video requests. It must take a large room at the LBJ Presidential Library in Texas to hold all the video programs recorded by WHCA.

My first time speaking to President Johnson directly involved a videotape request. It was in January 1969 on a Sunday morning. Weekend duty was normally slow with very few requests from the staff or Secret Service. Richard Nixon beat Hubert Humphrey in the November 1968 election and would be sworn in as the 37th President of the United States on the twentieth of January.

The telephone call directory lit up. The duty Officer office had direct lines to each WHCA Section and other key offices, which included a direct line to the Video Taping Section. When I answered the phone, the operator said for me to standby for a call from the President. Now, it probably was just a second or two but it seemed like minutes passed before Mr. Johnson came on the line. When your thirty years old working at the White House less than six months, my first thought was, what did I do wrong and how long will it take to pack up and transfer back to the Army.

Every terrible story told to me about their personal encounter with the President raced through my mind. When Mr. Johnson came on line, he said that his Press Secretary had been on a news show recently and asked if we had taped the program. Being of average intelligence and knowing misinformation could be deadly when talking to the President, I responded with I'm sure we did but could I check quickly and call him back. He said okay and that he was in the dining room of the residence. Like a flash, I punched up the direct line to the Video Taping Section and told the Technician on duty the President called asking to see the interview of his Press Secretary on one of the news show. He said they had taped the show and it would take a minute to find the tape and load the reel to play. I told him to go ahead and just clicked off when the phone rang.

In a few seconds, call director lit up again. My in stinks warned me the call wasn't going to be friendly. Sure enough, when I answered the call, the President was on the line. He said something to the effect that if we had the %@*@, #$#@% tape to put it on and if not to say so, then he hung up. I called the Ushers office and told them to tell the President the tape was ready on the closed circuit channel. Mr. Johnson must have had a lot on his mind his last week in office and wasn't going to wait on anyone, especially a WHCA Duty Officer.

Presidents like to travel and mingle with the people. Speaking to large crowds throughout the United States is something all of our Presidents seem to enjoy doing. President Johnson was no exception. However, demonstrators showing up at his speech sites were having an effect. He didn't want any advance publicity to where he was schedule to travel, which caused serious restrictions on pre-advance work normally necessary for a Presidential trip.

Establishing communications for the President, White House Staff, United States Secret Service and others, required a lot of communications equipment plus adequate manpower and time to install the equipment. The WHCA team dispatched on a military C-141 to Morgantown, West Virginia to support Mr. Johnson's visit required some major ingenuity On Maj Nelson's part as WHCA trip Officer. Lieutenant Commander Tom Coates and me were the Assistant Trip Officers. This was Tom Coates second trip and my first.

When the C-141 touched down at the Morgantown Municipal airport, a local newspaper reporter met us. He approached Maj Nelson and said a local rumor was floating around that Mr. Johnson was coming to Morgantown and were we from the White House. Ed told the reporter we were all military personnel from the Defense Communications Agency. He informed the reporter he had to get back to supervising the offloading of equipment, which was going to be set up and tested for the military. Now, that also was true so Ed was batting a hundred without divulging any info about the President's visit. Ed was one smooth WHCA Trip Officer. Tom Coates and I learned a lot from Ed on the Morgantown trip.

For a typical Presidential trip where the President would be making a few stops and speeches and then depart was referred to as an "In and Out" trip. Personnel normally consisted of a Trip Officer with one or two Assistant Trip Officers, depending on the number of speeches the President made. Around twenty enlisted personnel were required to set up and operate enough equipment, which basically extended the communications coverage at the White House to the trip site. A team leader was assigned to each communications element of the team, which normally consisted of a Switchboard, Radio, Telecommunications and Audio Visual Section. Later on a Administrative Assistant was added to help with logistics.

All of the equipment was offloaded on a rental truck. We proceeded to a downtown motel to wait on instructions to begin setting up for the President. Tom Coates and I were hanging around Ed's motel room waiting along with Ed on word that was okay to start setting up for the trip. We still didn't know if it was on or off. We were all lying around in the room doing nothing but waiting when the telephone rang. It was another reporter who had tracked Ed down looking for information on the President's trip. The reporter asked Ed what company we worked for. Ed replied DCA. "What are you doing in Morgantown with over twenty people and a plane load of equipment?" the reporter asked. "We're military personnel sent here on temporary duty to test communications equipment for DCA." Ed Replied. "Do you know anything about President Johnson coming to town and what he will be doing here when he arrives? "Don't know a thing", Ed replied. He was still batting a hundred in not telling a lie.

Around eleven P.M., WHCA Operations called to say the trip was a go. Ed was given the President's schedule and told he could start setting up for Mr. Johnson's arrival the next evening. Our team would have to work all night and the next day installing the equipment required for the President's visit. Ed briefed everyone on where President Johnson would speak and the motorcade route. Sense time was critical; the switchboard was installed at the local telephone company central office. Operations had already ordered in two direct lines from the White House Signal Switchboard and one direct Teletype circuit.

The WHCA Technicians knew what to do and how to do it once told the mission. It was amazing to see how efficient everyone performed their various duties. The radiomen worked all night installing radio base stations, which would provide the White House Staff and Secret Service a radio net they could interact with and also tie each radio back to the onsite switchboard. The Audio Visual team was instructed to install the necessary equipment for a speech on arrival at the airport and also at the hotel downtown. Maj Nelson assigned Tom Coates to supervise the airport site and told me to handle the downtown hotel site.

All the equipment for the President's arrival was installed and operational when Air Force One landed. Our trip site was ready for the President of the United States. Circuits back to the White House had been installed and telephone extensions to the airport for Air Force One and other extensions to the hotel speech site were ready. Our Radio Technicians double-checked the motorcade route to insure solid reception for the White House Staff and Secret Service.

The hand held radios built by Motorola was handed out to authorized users. The two-way radio was about the size of a brick. When a staff person said they already had a brick we knew what he was talking about. This was before circuit miniaturization was invented so we lugged around a lot of heavy equipment compared to what's on the market today.

Tom Coates handled the Airport stop and everything went off without a hitch. Ed rode in the motorcade to the downtown site. The speech site was in the ballroom of the hotel. Our A/V team checked out the sound system and installed two microphones on the podium. Two mikes were standard procedures. All audio visual equipment was installed with a complete redundant system. Should a piece of equipment become inoperative, the backup system automatically kicked in. Their audio recording equipment was about forty feet from the stage in front of where the President would be speaking. An audio multiply device specially built for the white house press was always connected to the podium microphones so the press could receive a live feed. This device, which was a portable Audio Multiple box, called a "Mult," contained numerous connections the press could plug into for a live audio feed from the presidential podium.

I was standing at stage right when the President entered. The Secret Service escorted him through the kitchen for security reasons. President Johnson stood next to where I was standing while the announcement, "Ladies and Gentlemen, the President of the United States", was made. He didn't speak to me and you know I didn't say a word to him. Johnson spoke for about ten minutes and departed for the airport. What a relief! Tom Coates couldn't say, "What a relief" until he heard over the radio net from the switchboard, "Wheels up on Air Force One". I'm sure the most relieved person was Ed Nelson. It was his trip. All the good things that happened at trip sites the Trip Officer could take credit. If something got fouled up, it was normally his head on the chopping block.

When the president of the United States travels outside of the white house, the communications capabilities provided at the white house are duplicated to wherever he travels. A trip out of country normally would require enough communications equipment to fill up a U.S. Air force Boeing C-141 cargo aircraft. Between twenty-five or thirty communicators would be required with skills in telecommunications, secure teletype and voice, manual operated two or three position switchboard and predetermined audio visual equipment for presidential speeches.

The audio visual department included men and women crossed trained in audio recording and mixing, sound amplification systems, stage lighting to include setting up the presidential lecture, presidential and U.S. flag and backdrop material. The John, Nixon, ford, and Carter administration used a blue backdrop. The presidential seal hung on the front of the podium was also part of our equipment requirements.

The presidential seal was another task that sometimes caused trip officers heartburn. We were instructed to wait until the president was announced to hang the seal on front of the podium. The person that hung the presidential seal was also responsible for making sure it was secured after the president finished speaking. Presidential seals made a nice memento and it was not uncommon for people to steal the seal. It happened only once for me.

The trip was Chicago, Illinois. There was a large crowd at the speech site and after the president finished his remarks, he stepped of stage and started shaking hands with those up front. Our presidential seal picker upper found it difficult to maneuver through the crowd of people and by the time he made it to the podium, the seal was missing. Just what I needed to ruin what had been a good trip without incident.

I asked him if he saw the person who snatched the seal. He said he thought it looked like someone in a maintenance uniform of some sort or a utility company employee. My best guess was that it was someone who worked at the hotel were the event took place or a telephone company employee. I contacted the hotel manager and my telephone company representative and informed them the presidential seal had been stolen and I had to report the theft to the FBI because it was a federal crime with serious consequences. I asked them to inform their employees that I was calling in the FBI but if the seal happened to show up the next morning, no charges would be filed.

The next morning I was called by the hotel and told that someone had dropped off a paper bag at the front desk addressed to white house. We had our presidential seal back and my bluff worked. To this day, I don't know if a law was broken if someone steals the presidential seal.

On the morning of January 20th, 1969, President Lyndon Johnson was scheduled to depart the White House premises for the last time as President of the United States. At 12 o'clock noon, Richard Nixon would be sworn in as our 37th President. It was around ten a.m. when the phone rang at my Duty Officer desk. Two maintenance personnel from Electronic Maintenance were letting me know they were on their way to the oval office to remove the "three eyed monster" and the Associated Press (AP), United Press International (UPI) and Reuters Teletype machines were two pieces of equipment especially engineered for Mr. Johnson by the Electronic Maintenance personnel of WHCA. Our operations Division was told by the incoming Nixon administration to make sure these items were removed immediately from the oval office before Nixon arrived at his new office.

The "three eyed monster", was a fancy television console with three, twenty-one inch picture tubes. A remote was especially designed so that LBJ could have all three major networks on at once. He could flip back and forth to activate the sound on whichever screen caught his fancy. ABC, CBS and NBC were the only networks around in the sixties.

The AP, UPI and Reuter's printers were placed inside a single cabinet with all three-news printers printing out current world news. The cabinet was sound proofed to eliminate the clatter of the Teletype printers. Mr. Johnson was an avid reader and insisted on first hand news information His method of governing was to go to the source instead of using his staff.

Shortly after the phone call from the electronic maintenance technicians who were headed to the oval office, I received another phone call from President Johnson's staff. The gist of the message was no equipment would be removed from the White House until after 12 noon. Mr. Johnson was still the President and to keep our #$%*&## technicians out of the oval office. We were trying to be efficient. Johnson's staff was letting us know they were still in control and would remain so up to the last second of the Johnson Administration.

Chapter 16

Nixon Administration

At twelve noon on January 20, 1969, Richard Nixon raised his right hand and took the following oath of office. "I do solemnly swear that I will faithfully execute the office of President of the United States, and will to the best of my ability, preserve, protect and defend the Constitution of the United States, so help me God"

Robert (Bob) Haldeman and John Ehrlichman were President Nixon's closest advisors. Haldeman was appointed Chief Of Staff and Ehrlichman Counselor to the President for Domestic Affairs. Whereas Mr. Johnson was a hands on type president, we were to find out Mr. Nixon delegated a tremendous amount of authority to Haldeman and Ehrlichman. Haldeman was the man who pulled our chain. When he or his twenty-three year old assistant barked, we jumped. That's the way politics works. Young volunteer campaign workers who picked the winning candidate ended up with plush government jobs. It didn't really matter if they knew the least thing about what they were supposed to do. The winner takes the spoils of government jobs both high ranking and low ranking. It is practiced by Republicans and Democrats and continues today.

On January 20th when the incoming president-elect takes the oath of office, thousands of high ranking political appointees are replaced by the incoming administration. It is a massive moving day for those holding jobs designated by the Civil Service Administration for political appointments. This practice occurs for Republicans and Democrats. This may be a tipoff why things are so out of whack at the highest echelons of our government.

One of the first things WHCA was ordered to do was dismantle the Top Secret audio taping system installed for LBJ at his direction. It was one of the duties I was briefed on when first assigned as a Duty Officer. Only a handful of personnel in WHCA were aware of the taping system. Duty Officers had to know because someone from Mr. Johnson's immediate staff would call when the tapes needed changing. The recorder in the Oval office was Charlie Brown One and the cabinet room, Charlie Brown Two. When the president's personal secretary called, she simple said, "please check Charlie Brown One or whichever system required attention. That was our signal to call a designated person from the Audio Visual section to go up and change the tapes.

Rumors were floating around that the incoming Nixon administration was told that WHCA wasn't trustworthy. Our switchboard operators supposedly listened in on conversations and since all were active duty military, their loyalty were to the Pentagon, according to their inside information. None of these rumors were true. It was a blatant lie someone was using to build up their own self importance with the new administration.

Every effort was taken in our recruitment process to insure that the men and women selected were aware of our responsibilities and honored to be serving the Commander In Chief of the United States of America, regardless of political views. All military personnel assigned to the Agency wore civilian suits while assigned at the White House. Military uniforms could not be worn on duty except on the occasion of a promotion or personal award presentation.

Every member of the Agency observed military protocol when dealing internally within the Agency. Externally, we didn't address ourselves by our military rank or title. It offered some unique challenges sometimes for our newly assigned senior enlisted personnel and officers. For example, when a communications support team was assembled to support an upcoming Presidential trip, experience verses rank determined who was in charge. Each person assigned to the Agency underwent a strenuous training program before being authorized to serve as Team Chief or Trip Officer. This method of operation was unique but effective. However, it was not the way the military normally conducted business. The enlisted men and women assigned to the Agency were individually selected and the best of the best in my opinion. They came from the Army, Air Force, Navy, Marine Corps and Coast Guard. During my tour of duty, I had a Navy boss, Air Force boss, Army boss and Marine boss. It may appear like I couldn't hold a job for a long period of time in the Agency.

Spending time worrying about training, moral or discipline problems took up very little time for those in leadership positions. On those few and far between cases where someone broke established standards, they were immediately processed back to their respective branch of service, sometimes with orders reflecting a departure date before the incident occurred. We focused all our energies on insuring that all communication facilities were installed and operational based on the President's itinerary for the specific trip site.

Politics played no part in what we did or how we did it. Democrats and Republicans were provided the same professional service.

President Johnson did not like any advance publicity on his trips so the advance work required was done in secret, which limited installing communication systems until the last minute.

President Nixon, we found out, did not operate in the same fashion. Our Operations department was briefed on requirements well in advance. An expanded White House Trip Advance Office assembled members from various departments required to support a Presidential Trip. A pre-advance team would travel to the designated city or site to determine logistical and manpower requirements.

A typical pre-advance team consisted of a representative from the White House Advance office, United States Secret Service (USSS), White House Press Office, WHCA, and a Air Force One Advance Representative. Each member was responsible for determining specific requirements for their departments so that necessary logistics could be arranged. My Trip Officer experience up this point consisted of the one trip to Morgantown, West Virginia. It would take many more trips and a lot of hands on training before Operations scheduled you for your first check ride trip. The easiest and least complicated was being designated to provide communications for the President on a trip inside Washington, D.C. or suburbs. Normally it consisted of one Officer and around two or three enlisted technicians to provide support for that particular event.

My first trip in which I was in charge of communications was a trip to the Sheraton Hotel in Washington, D.C. I met the Secret Service Lead Agent, the Staff and Press Advance at the Sheraton to check out preliminary requirements.

President Nixon was scheduled to speak at the National Business Association luncheon. Once the decision was made as to how and where the President would enter the hotel and the location for the

Presidential podium, I was ready to call Operations and give them my personnel and equipment requirements.

Radio coverage was no problem because we could communicate back to the White House on the radio net permanently installed to cover Washington, D.C. Three portable radios were set up by the radio technicians to cover the two nets required by Secret Service and the one net required by the White House Staff. The two A/V technicians brought the podium, backdrop, flags, and their audio equipment. A local telephone representative would be available to order a handful of extensions off the White House Signal Switchboard.

No matter where the President was going, the Staff Advance always selected a room on site, which the President could use. This room was called the holding room for the president. An extension off the White House switchboard was installed and if the staff Advance wanted to keep his job, a bathroom was available for the President's use.

One of the requirements at a trip site was to insure there was an announcement microphone installed and available to announce the President when he arrived. It is an impressive event to have a huge ballroom filled with thousands of people and right before the president makes his entrance, you here ruffles and flourishes then the announcement, "Ladies and gentlemen, the President of The United States". Butterflies were known to flutter about when I was the designated announcer. It basically wasn't a big deal but we probably had more flaps caused from something going wrong during the announcement than anything else.

A few weeks after president Nixon resigned, President Ford was being announced when the young man making the announcement said, "ladies and gentlemen, the president of the united states and Mrs. Nixon." Ford was a very tolerant man and the technician did not lose his job.

The adage to take care of the little things because the big things will take care of themselves proved to be true on numerous occasions during my tour of duty at the white house.

When President Nixon arrived for the event, he was escorted from the motorcade through a back entrance, straight to the holding room. It was my first time being in the same room with Mr. Nixon. The Staff Advance started briefing the President on what was happening. He explained that the band would play ruffles and flourishes and then he would be announced. The announce mike was standing next to the entrance door to the ballroom. I had one of the AV technicians standing by to make the announcement. This being my first trip as the Trip Officer I wasn't taking any chances on blowing the announcement.

The President was told that there were around twenty-five hundred from the National Business Association. He would inter from stage right and proceed to the center of the stage where the presidential podium was located. I also heard him tell the President that there were two TV cameras filming. One located off stage right and the other off stage left. The band struck up ruffles and flourishes then the announcement was made. Mr. Nixon spoke for about twenty minutes. At the conclusion of his speech, Mr. Nixon departed for the White House. My first "in-town" trip was accomplished without incident and so I still had a job.

The day-to-day duties as a Duty Officer can best be summed up as a lot of boredom mixed in with a mixture of total panic. A typical duty cycle could be described as exciting as watching an action movie with no sound when suddenly, it seemed everyone in the White House Complex had some sort of communications request. Our workload increased dramatically when advance teams were deployed working at trip sites for forthcoming presidential travel. Our office was manned twenty-four hours a day and functioned as a round the clock coordination center for the Operations Department.

After almost four years as a Duty Officer, I was selected to replace another Warrant Officer who had been Project Coordinator for the massive communications facility upgrade ongoing at the White House.

This was the beginning of the computer age which meant every piece of communications equipment installed in the basement of the White House had to be replaced with the latest and most efficient equipment available. The tricky part was our present system had to remain operational continuously at the same time the new system was being installed; in the same location. My days working a twenty-four hour a day shift schedule was over.

The White House has direct circuits to all major departments of our government. To name a few were the State Department, Federal Bureau of Investigation (FBI), Central Intelligence Agency (CIA),

National Security Agency (NSA), Department of Defense (Pentagon), Director of Intelligence (DIA) and direct hot lines to Russia and other countries. For two years my duties were to be directly responsible for the Top Secret cryptographic codes and equipment used at the White House.

Every six months I had the task of flying to Japan and the other countries with a direct link to the white house to upgrade the codes. I'm hesitant to list the other countries because the information may still be classified and I'm too old to go to jail at this stage of my life. I was always accompanied by one of my senior enlisted men. I was armed with a snub noised 38 caliber pistol just in case a spy attempted to steal the codes. We had diplomatic pass ports and flew first class. When we presented our diplomatic passports at the airport terminal, we were escorted directly to the waiting aircraft without a body a body scan or search.

My first trip out of country was to Paris, France. President Nixon had been sworn into office January 20, 1969, and this would be his first trip to meet the heads of state of other countries.

Advance teams of secret service agents, white house staff, press and communications teams were dispatched in advance to prepare for president Nixon's arrival. Senior officers were in charge so this was a look, watch, and ask questions type trip for me and another training officer.

Paris, France is a beautiful city with an abundance of historical buildings and artifacts. The Eiffel tower and the Arc de Triomphe historical structures were awesome when viewed up close and personal. Unlike America where we have a tendency to tear down and rebuild, Paris is a city of century old buildings. The hotel De Crillon which is a five star hotel was located across the street from the American Embassy and used by all staff advance personnel during the trip. The hotel was built in the 18th century and was loaded with historical significance. Going from living on a small farm with no electric power, running water or indoor bathroom, this was quite a leap for this South Georgian.

President Charles De Gaulle was president of France during this period of time. When Air Force One touched down at the Paris International airport, De Gaulle was on hand to great Nixon and welcomes him to France. Although I had seen photos of him, he was a lot taller than I had imagined. His welcoming remarks were in French even though De Gaulle spoke excellent English. It was probably De Gaulle that convinced most French people to converse with foreigners in their native tongue and not English even though all French children are taught English in school and can speak the language.

One event was scheduled to take place at the Palace Versailles, the French royal Jewell and showcase for the world. History teaches that in 1660, Louis XIV, coming to the throne and taking on full royal powers, was looking for a place outside the city of Paris where he could travel and relax. In 1682 the palace was completed and Louis XIV took up residence. There must have been a shortage of paint colors because the entire structure is done in gold, real gold. We spent a good day establishing communication links back to our hub installed at the hotel De Crillon in Paris.

My next presidential trip to Paris was when President Georges Pompidou died in 1974. I was on my way home from work late one evening when I received a call on our radio network. My instructions were to leave immediately for Andrews Air Force Base. Our home in Woodbridge, VA was twenty-three miles one way but I was almost home when I got the call. I hung up and called Marian to pack my bags and would fill her in on the details when I arrived. Before I could tell her anything, I had to call our operations center to find out myself.

That's when I found out Nixon would be going to the state funeral in Paris.

The advance team for the 1969 trip to Paris had ten days to complete on the ground work required for a presidential trip. I was told we had one day and one night to complete everything for this trip. Our flight on the backup Air Force One departed the airport around 11 P.M. Instead of sleeping on the plane, I would be making numerous phone calls from the elaborate communications capabilities of Air Force One to the American Embassy and issuing instructions to them so that they could relay the orders to the French telephone Company.

Myself and one other Communications officer was on the aircraft and we had about a six hour head start to establish locations for our equipment, storage facilities, hotel accommodations, and make arrangements for one large truck to haul the equipment in and five rental vehicles required for our use in Paris.

The communications equipment along with twenty technicians and two more officers arrived in late evening on an Air Force C-141. Once on the ground, we had one night to complete our work before the president arrived. The good news was that Nixon would not be making any public remarks so we didn't have to worry about any speech sites and audio visual requirements. Off the cuff remarks that could be made without prior planning was always handled by one of our audio visual technicians that traveled with the white house press corps.

This individual was equipped with a portable Swiss made Nagra tape recorder that had a shotgun type microphone attached. The trip went off without a major flap so we all got to keep our jobs. What a way to make a living.

A presidential announcement was also one of our areas of responsibly. It could be as simple as saying, "ladies and gentlemen, the president of the United States." Or as complicated as announcing three foreign dignitaries with names impossible to pronounce and getting the coordination down between the announcement and the band director. Band Directors need enough prior warning to bring the band members to attention. The actual event goes like this; the band is called to attention and then he gives the signal for ruffles and flourishes. Ruffles and flourishes are played three times then the announcement is made and hail to the chief is played.

An announce microphone was installed back stage at the entrance the president would be arriving and an intercom between the person making the announcement and the band director would be installed. Trip Officers with experience knew to rehearse this simple task with the band prior to the event to insure everybody knew when and what was occurring.

No matter what the experience level or how many times simple tasks or practiced, things can and will cause events to happen that could not have been imagined. The most famous snafu occurred in New Orleans with one of our more experienced officers.

President Nixon was scheduled be make a speech in the city auditorium with over 2000 attendees. The simple task of making sure the announce microphone was switched off until the event began, was overlooked. Probably because of last minute changes that frequently occurred on all trips,

All advance team personnel including White House Staff, Secret Service agents and Communications Trip Officers were equipped with small radios worn on their hip and hooked to their belt. A small wire connected to a microphone was ran up our coat sleeve and held in our hand for transmitting. A special made molded ear pieces that fit in the ear cavity was connected to hear transmissions. This helped somewhat in limiting calling attention to ourselves so that we could do our jobs without people staring at us.

When the motorcade was about two minutes from arriving, the lead white house staff advance would signal, "two minutes." This signal alerted the advance team to get ready. The officer who would be making the announcement relayed the message to the band director over his intercom with him.

For a reason only the band director and God knows, the next thing you hear is the band playing ruffles and flourishes. The president is still in the motorcade. "Hold it, hold it, screamed the trip officer. Don't play until I give you the signal just like we rehearsed, you dump 5$3@*&^! The next thing heard is 2000 people in the auditorium breaking out into laughter and giggles. With the announce microphone swathed on and hot, the sound is being broadcast over the sound system. The president finally arrives and the band director is told over the intercom to play ruffles and flourishes. "Play ruffles and flourishes now!" He's told. Unfortunately this simple little oversight caused a lot of restless nights for a few people. It adds strength to the saying that we should pay close attention to the little things in life because the big things will take care of themselves. The other major duty was to be the fall guy if anything went wrong, which did happen on occasion.

Every person assigned to WHCA has two primary jobs. Their first job is in the department or section in which they have been trained. Most of the electronic equipment used by The White House Communications Agency was off the shelf commercial equipment or specifically designed equipment made especially for the Agency. This required that everybody assigned had to be given specific training in the equipment and its use.

The majority of the radio equipment was manufactured by Motorola. The concept for the cellular phones predominate in use today was the same system that we installed at presidential trip sites in the sixties. I was told that the first working system was designed by a WHCA technician. True of not, our use of technology to provide a communications capability not in use anywhere else, provided an unheard of service for the White House Staff and Secret Service.

The office of president of the United States demands the best communications system available. The best system is what our agency provided no matter where the president traveled. We were good at what we did and sometimes, a situation would present itself where we could impress folks with how smart we were. That opportunity occurred for me on a trip to Bermuda.

Presidential trips to other countries were more complex and required longer to establish the necessary communications on location and tied back to the White House. The trip to Bermuda was such a trip. Prime Minister Edward Heath of Great Brittan invited Mr. Nixon to a state dinner during his visit to the British Commonwealth. The event was a black tie, Head of State, event scheduled to take place on a beautiful British ship, Her Majesty's Navy, docked in the harbor.

Once the advance team arrived in Bermuda, immediate contact was made with the ship's captain so that the details of the state dinner could be agreed too and pre-advance trip personnel could complete the necessary pre-advance work required by the White House staff, Secret Service, and establishing the necessary communications for the presidential trip, could begin.

At the first meeting which was held at the captain's mast on board the ship, everyone was introduced and we paired up with our counterparts so that every little detail could be worked out in advance. The ships communications officer was our contact. He was cordial, and somewhat cocky when describing how elaborate and complex British communications were on the ship. The ship's captain was very specific during the meeting when he reminded everyone that he was the captain and that his people were responsible for everything that occurred, on ship, during the visit.

Late one evening after a long day and hungry because we hadn't eaten all day, we walked over to a small café a couple of blocks from the ship to catch a bite to eat. The senior British Communications officer tagged along. While waiting for our food, I received a radio call from the White House Duty Officer. When the conversation ended, the British chap asked who was I talking too because he thought he heard me say the White House and he knew that a small radio I was using, was a line of site transmitting and receiving device, so it was impossible for me to reach to the White House. I explained to him that I was talking to the White House and that we used complex multiplexing equipment to extend the audio signal beyond its limited reach. Although the nice chap didn't say anything in so many words, it was obvious from the expression on his face that he was in communications, and I was feeding him a bunch of bull. "Are you married, I asked him?" "Why, yes I am. We have two beautiful children and live in a flat approximately twenty kilometers outside London." "Although its early morning in England, if you will give me your house phone number, I'll her on the radio for you." I could tell from his expression that he was beginning to feel we Americans told a lot of whoppers. I called the White House switchboard and asked them to dial a number for me in England. The operator said to standby while he made the connection. In a few moments, I heard the phone ringing and then a very sleepy British voice of a female say, hello. Then I said, "Hold on a second please, your hubby would like to speak to you," and handed him the radio. He never asked how I did it and I certainly did not volunteer the information. There may be an old, retired British Officer wandering around England mumbling to himself, "I wonder how he did that?'

As the trip unfolded, every individual on the advance team and senior White House staff members for the president received a lesson in diplomatic protocol on things not to do when dealing with Her Majesties Navy.

When the president traveled to other countries, it was customary for the host nation to allow our audio visual technicians to furnish the microphones and provide the audio for our own recording and an audio feed to the national news media. This may have been customary but the British Navy was having no part of allowing this to happen on their ship.

Unfortunately, there are a few high ranking people who worked at the White House who feel they can dictate to others no matter where they are. A telephone call was made back to the White House complaining of the fact the British Navy was playing hardball and asked someone to contact the Prime Minister's office and obtain permission to use our technicians and microphones on the ship. A compromise was worked out so that even though our technicians were not on board the ship, we would be receiving a live audio feed to pipe to the news media.

It was a black tie affair which required everyone involved to be dressed appropriately in a black tuxedo, even though we were not allowed on deck during the state dinner.

After being introduced by the Prime Minister, Mr. Nixon began his speech by saying, "I could well respond to the Prime Minister's remarks by saying, as I can, with great conviction, that I agree with every word that he has uttered. However, I think the occasion demands a bit more than that because of its historic significance, and so it is important on such an occasion that I, on my part, state on behalf of all of our officials who are here, our appreciation for the hospitality that has been extended and our hopes for the future as that future will be affected by this meeting.

First, I think we will all agree that we could not have selected a better place in which to meet, as far as its historical significance. The Prime Minister had some marvelous historical anecdotes with regard to Bermuda. I think the best one that our staff was able to think up was one from Mark Twain. Mark Twain once visited Bermuda, and he said to a friend at the conclusion of his visit, he said, "You may want to go to heaven, but I would rather stay here." So the closest thing to heaven, certainly on this earth and this hemisphere, on such an occasion like this, is Bermuda.

Then, too, the place that we are meeting, this beautiful ship, the fact that it is Her Majesty's Navy, it seems to me, that that choice must have been made when the Prime Minister did his usual careful checking of the backgrounds of those who would be here—not only the President of the United States and his guests, the Secretary of State and the Secretary of the Treasury, were all former naval people." The president made a remarkable speech; unfortunately, we were not receiving a single word of what he was saying.

Recording equipment and an audio multiple for the press, was installed at the foot of the gangplank going up to the ship. We were receiving a clean audio feed provided by the British Navy and Prime Minister Heath was introducing Mr. Nixon.

When President Nixon began his remarks, suddenly, a high pitched audio signal appeared over the technicians head sets. The news media began screaming and shouting that their sound feed was terrible and to fix the problem immediately. Naturally, the White House staff shimmed in with more insults in language reserved for backyard playgrounds from kids whose mamas didn't wash their mouth out with soup the first time they used such language.

As soon as the speeches ended, suddenly, the sound was nice and clear again. The communications officer was all apologetic when he told us how sorry he was for the lousy audio feed, but we should have no fear, his technicians had a perfect copy of the complete program and they were making us a copy as he spoke. The lesson learned was, do not try to out fox a fox when invited to his henhouse for dinner.

Chapter 17

Watergate

On June 7, 1972, five burglars were arrested at the Democratic National Committee headquarters, located in the Watergate complex in Washington, D.C. These men were not ordinary criminals looking for cash. They were all hired by the Committee to Elect Richard Nixon for a second term as president. To confront the daily onslaught of bad news, the president traveled throughout the United States and also to the Middle East, Europe and Russia, to tell his side of the story about the Watergate break-in. The white house called these speeches Operation Candor. They were designed to let the president explain to the American people, and also to the world, that he was on the job, and taking care of the nations business. Watergate was just a overblown story that the news media used to increase their ratings. His poll numbers were down around the trash can level. I participated in two of these trips as the communications Trip Officer.

The first was a trip to Houston, Texas where a white house press conference was scheduled. The advance team included secret service, press, white house advance coordinators and my communication team of twenty-one personnel, plus an aircraft load of communications equipment.

The news conference was to be held at the civic center in downtown Houston. A large crowed of invited guests selected and screened by the white house advance team filled the auditorium. The audio visual technicians installed four stand-up microphones on the stage, which led back to their sound mixer and master feed for the news media. Chairs for the White House press were placed on the stage so that they could be seated until the president called for them to ask their question.

When the presidential motorcade arrived, I was standing at stage right where an announce microphone had been placed to announce his arrival on stage. It was normal procedures for the lead White House advance person to brief the president on what to expect when he went on stage. The president was told that the podium with the presidential seal was located at center stage. The news media would be seated on the stage and when called on by name, stand and ask their question which usually was a detailed question and follow-up question.

Dan Rather was the White House correspondent for CBS news and was selected to ask the first question. Normally, press protocol dictated the senior correspondent, who was Helen Thomas from UPI, would ask the first question but protocol was not followed for this press conference.

Once briefed, he was announced, "Ladies and gentlemen, the President of the United State," without the customary ruffles and flourishes and hail to the chief protocol. Nixon briskly walked up to the podium and said that he had some brief remarks to make before taking the first question.

Suddenly I heard in my earpiece, "Gill, what is your location?" It was the radio console controller directing radio traffic for staff and secret service for the trip. "I'm at stage right, I said." "Go to stage left immediately."

Stage left was where the audio visual technicians' were controlling the sound system and national new media feed for the networks. The press conference was going out live on all the major television networks.

I walked behind the stage curtain to where the sound system and audio feeds were installed. I didn't have to say a word to know what was wrong because the senior technician was down under the table where the equipment was installed pulling on cables. Things like that don't happen when everything is going smoothly.

General Adams, who was commander of WHCA, was already at the table when I arrived. He always traveled with the president on Air Force One to trip sites. Adams leaned over and told me that there was no power going to the standup microphones on stage. He then grabbed me by the shoulder and we quickly ran toward the network television truck that was carrying the live feed to all the networks.

My heart must have missed some beats because I could see flashing before my eyes my career at the White House ruined. Millions of people watching the news conference on television would not be able to hear any of the questions being asked. It was my responsibility to insure that all communications worked properly. All was not well with the floor microphones. They were dead without power. So was I if those microphones didn't work.

Thank God my special angel did not run off and leave me to die a thousand deaths. My brain kicked back into gear so I spun around and ran back inside. The problem had to be somewhere around the console we installed because all the feeds were going into our equipment and then out to the networks.

On this trip, a young man who was making his first trip as an audio technician was there to observe and learn. It would take a lot of trips and plenty of training before he was qualified to handle the job as the lead audio technician.

The senior technician was in total panic mode and this young man probably thought these type of malfunctions happened all the time. Besides, he was not responsible for anything so why be shook up.

I asked him, "son, do you have any idea were the problem is?" "Somebody must have kicked the power junction providing power to the microphones, he said." The mixer meters indicate that all the mikes are dead. The president was still speaking but I knew at any moment he would finish his remarks and begin the news conference.

I ordered him to crawl out on the stage and check the junction box. He was small enough to slide through the legs of the chairs. "Sir, you want me to crawl out there while the president is speaking and those people are watching?" Yes, right now!

He immediately crawled out through the legs of the chairs until he reached the junction box. Once the power cord for the microphones were plugged back in, bingo! They were now operational. Nixon finished his remarks and called on Dan Rather for the first question. My military career was saved by a young man I didn't know. I wish I could remember his name. To me he will always be known as my special angel sent by God.

My other trip in June, 1974, was to the small city of Yalta, located on the Black sea, in the Soviet Union. The Yalta conference was held February, 1945 and brought together the Big Three Allied leaders; Stalin, Churchill and Roosevelt. Because of political decisions that were made in 1945, which were still very controversial in political circles, the name Yalta was never used by the Nixon Administration. Yalta was situated in the Crimea territory of Russia so all references referred to Crimea instead of Yalta. The White House Advance party of staff, Secret Service and Communication personnel were all located in a five story hotel in Yalta which was completely emptied for our exclusive use. All meals were consumed on premise with very little choice for what we ate. Whereas we drink sweet tea in South Georgia, the Russians drink vodka, lots of vodka. It was consumed at all meals and at all meetings I had with their representatives. Alcohol addiction was prevalent throughout the Soviet Empire and in my opinion, played a major role the collapse of Soviet Empire in the late eighties. First rate products can't be produced by people who are intoxicated with booze.

A young lady who spoke perfect British English was assigned as my translator. My instincts told me she was a KGB intelligence agent assigned to try and gain whatever sliver of intelligence she could from me and our technicians. When I spoke to her in my normal cadence with a pronounced southern drawl, she complained to me that I didn't speak English like she was taught. I had to develop a deliberate method of slowly pronouncing each word I spoke to be understood by her. After fourteen days of talking like that, when I got back home, my wife told me she spoke English and I didn't have to pronounce each word for her. I traded one of our phones for a Russian made phone and was showing it to my wife. After holding it for a second she said it sure didn't appear to be well made. "Don't worry any more about the outcome if we ever go to war with Russia, everything I saw that they make was inferior to our equipment," I said.

Dealing with the Russian technicians and employees who worked at the hotel, taught me that although there may be vast ideological difference between governments, people all over the world strive for the same basic goals in life.

Chapter 18

Burn Out

Politics can be a ruthless, cutthroat business and Watergate provided the knife to start the blood flowing. President Nixon handed the democrats the perfect tool to end his administration. Thankfully, my job was to provide the president with the best communications possible and our agency didn't care what political party was in power.

After six years being assigned to WHCA, I was beginning to feel burned out. The long hours and numerous trips were taking a toll. Marian never complained about the long hours and frequent trips but I knew that having to raise two daughters without much input from me, was above and beyond the normal duties of a wife and mother.

Juliann would be turning thirteen in October, 1974. She had grown up to be a beautiful, articulate young teenager with a twinkle in her eye. The braces on her teeth didn't hinder her smile at all.

Elizabeth was ten years old and just as pretty. Beth knew she was the baby in the family and at times tried to take advantage of her special position of being the baby. After church on Sundays, we would go to a local restaurant for lunch. On this occasion, we had ordered a pork shop meal. Marian told the waitress to bring the girls a child's plate which was the same dish as ours except they had one pork shop instead of two.

When our meal was served, Beth looked over the plates and immediately started whining. "I only have one pork shop and you have two, she said." Like a good mother, Marian told her to hush and proceeded to share her other pork shop with Beth.

In two years, I would be eligible for retirement. After a considerable amount of prayer, I decided to ask for a regular assignment back to the Army. My suits were beginning to look worn and I would have to purchase a new set of military uniforms to wear now that I was going back to the regular army.

My request was approved and I received orders back to Fort Gordon, Georgia where we lived when we got married in 1959. My new job would be in the Training and Doctrine Command at the Signal School.

Chapter 19

How to write a book and keep a secret

As a Warrant Officer, my military specialty was in telecommunications as a cryptographer. The department where I worked was responsible for insuring Army field manuals in telecommunications were incorporated correctly. A massive rewrite was taking place to bring the manuals up to date. The only writing that I had done lately was writing letters to Marian when I was in Vietnam in 1966-1967.

There are many a day I wish I had paid closer attention in class when Mrs. Martha Harrison was describing sentence structure and the difference between nouns and pronouns at Blackshear High school.

My boss was an army colonel who majored in English in college. There was more civilian civil service employess working in the department than military personnel. The majority had master's degree in English with the daily job of editing field manuals being written. I was tasked with rewriting a field manual named "Standing Operation Instructions" which described how to use the code books issued to infantry units. The manual was written in the same dry, dull, why must I read this manual method used during World War II.

The only guidance I received was when I asked the colonel what the objective for the rewrite was other than making sure the procedures reflected the current method of operations. "Have you ever read a army field manual? Have you ever read a copy of Newsweek or Time magazine? Which would you rather read? He asked.

Being of sound mind and limited intelligence, I said the news magazines. "Okay, that's your assignment. Turn that army gobble gook into an interesting to read field manual." I knew what to do but how was I going to pull off such an assignment with a limited background in writing and an "I slept through my English class" level of understanding on how to write.

After spending days rewriting and verifying the correct operating procedures, I turned over my rough draft to a civilian proof reader and editor. He had been a civil service employee for years and very capable in his job. My boss was leaning on me to complete the assignment as soon as possible. I found out the task of updating and rewriting the manual had been in process for over two years. That was plain ridiculous but the good news was it couldn't be blamed on me in that I had only been working on it a few weeks.

After returning some of my work my editor said that I was doing a good job and to keep it up. I told him, "This isn't my line of work. I slept through English classes and do a poor job of sentence structure." His comments next have remained with me over the years. "Don't worry about editing you own work. That's my job. This building is full of editors like me with masters degrees in English but we only have a handful of people that can write in a style people enjoy reading." If he was trying to say things to make me feel good, then his mission was successful.

If God was grading Christians based on their church attendance record, I would be rated a D minus during my assignment at the White House. The long hours and constant travel was used as an excuse to miss church on more Sundays than I care to mention.

After buying a house in the Martinez community of Augusta, Georgia, finding a church home became our number one priority. Several churches were visited until it became obvious we belonged at Abilene Baptist. Juliann and Elizabeth became Christians and were baptized at Abilene. No longer was there a flimsy excuse for missing a service unless a family member was sick. It was also the church where I was ordained as a deacon. It was an honor I've never felt worthy of.

My new job was from seven in the morning until four thirty in the afternoon. No overtime required. My office was on the fifth floor of Signal Towers. At four thirty P.M., there was such a rush to leave the building all elevators were in constant use. The long hours were over for a while and being on constant standby at all times of the day was a thing of the past.

After a year, the Field Manual was finished and sent to the press. Checking other manuals for cryptographic security input was a boring job. Different departs of Training and Doctrine Command was constantly trying to outdo each other with innovated methods for getting the message of improved security techniques incorporated in the manuals for the troops to read. I mentioned to my boss why not a manual on "How to Keep a Secret." Our job was insuring the numerous methods of communicating were done in such a manner the enemy could listen all day and not glean a sliver of intelligence. My orders were to go for it.

Writing and researching documents requires and extensive data base for research analysis. The Signal School had one of the best research libraries in the army. It was located on the ground floor in the building where I worked. The library contained official military records of major battles fought by our soldiers.

Reviewing after actions reports prepared by commanders in the field in Vietnam was a treasure trove of information in intelligence and communications security. After action reports were used to document past actions and their outcome. Commanders would also list the things that worked and the things that didn't work which provided a wealth of information for my new task of writing, "How to Keep a Secret."

Working eight hour days at the office, spending time with my wife and children when not at work, was the highlight every day. Our family discussions at the dinner table at meal time were the perfect setting to hear the girls describe their day at school. Both took after their mother and made good grades.

Waycross and Blackshear was a four hour drive from our home so every month we drove home on the week-end to visit our parents. I didn't know life good be so enjoyable without all the stress but once again, things have a way of changing, and sometime not like we plan

Chapter 20

Gerald Ford Administration

President Nixon had resigned the office of president and Gerald Ford, who Nixon appointed Vice President, was sworn in as president. The war in Vietnam was finally coming to an end for American troops. President Ford made the political decision to pardon Nixon for all past and future activities relating to Watergate even though he had not been indicted.

Ford told the American people in a nationwide television broadcast that it was time to put this chapter in the history books so that our government could once again get back to governing for the people. That one action dropped Ford's polling numbers drastically and democrats could smell victory in the next general election.

I had been tipped off that the assignment desk at the pentagon was ready to notify me that my next assignment would be in Korea. I had not completed twenty years so when the orders came, I would have to salute and go. There are no, "I don't want to go options" in the military.

After receiving the disturbing news about having to go to Korea, I called the personnel director at WHCA and asked if they could use some help. I was rested up and ready to go. He placed me on hold for a moment than came back on line and asked if I could be at the White House the next day to be interviewed by their new commander who didn't know me from a sign post.

I flew to Washington, D.C. the next day to be interviewed by the new commander for the assignment. General Riley was very cordial during the interview and flattered me with comments on what a good reputation I had from my previous assignment to WHCA. My good friend Ron Thompsen was a fellow warrant officer who was the Assistant Operations Officer for the Agency. Ron had taken a job with the Secret Service Communication Department and was retiring at the end of the month.

General Riley told me he wanted me take Ron's place when he retired at the end of the month. "This may cause come hard feelings for you from the warrant officers currently serving as Duty Officers. As you know, under normal circumstances, the senior warrant officer on the desk would be eligible for any position that opened up. I need someone with your experience in this position."

I told him I understood because I served for almost four years as a Duty Officer but he was the commander and if he felt I was the best qualified for the job, so be it. Official orders assigning me back to the Agency were waiting for me the next day. The Gill family was headed back to Washington, D.C.,

Chapter 21

Gerald Ford, Jimmy Carter
Presidential Debate

Cobwebs had developed around my brain from eight hour work days at Ft. Gordon. Providing communications for the Commander in Chief of our country requires dedication, stamina, knowledge of what's required and the ability work under pressure and think clearly. It only took one trip on a presidential trip site to snap me back to reality on what to do and how to do it. The mission was simple; provide the president the best communications possible.

The first and only debate between President Ford and Governor Jimmy Carter was scheduled to occur on September 23, 1976 at the Walnut theatre in Philadelphia, PA. Philadelphia is only a short distance from D.C. so we drove up in rental cars and a truck load of communications equipment. It was a easy tip to prepare for with the debate at the Walnut theatre and a campaign rally for Ford after the speech. Debate coordinators from President Ford and Carter met numerous times before the debate to work out logistics and cosmetic staging that would be used.

To make the staging as static as possible, the president would not use the customary podium with the presidential seal. Instead, two identical podiums provided by the theatre would be used. Stage lighting and sound would be provided the television network providing the live feed for broadcast by all the networks. To cut down on expense, this arrangement was used frequently by the three major networks. ABC news was selected to broadcast the audio and video feed which would be aired live.

Because the presidential podium was not being used, ABC provided the audio from both podiums to the networks. The audio visual technicians simply set up their recorders and recorded the debate because the network was controlling the debate and not the White House Communications Agency. A major technical blunder was about to take place and all the blame belonged to ABC news technical personnel.

The debate began on time and was proceeding without incident from a technical point of view. Politically, Both Ford and Carter stumbled when they responded to some of the questions being asked by the news panel selected to ask the questions. Ford tried to defend his flub when he said there were no communist in Poland and Carter was taken to task about his Playboy interview.

Suddenly, the audio system failed. Everyone watching the debate on television could see the debate taking place but there was no sound. Our internal radio net lit up like a Christmas tree with audio traffic from the White Staff and Secret Service asking what was the problem. The senior staff was screaming for WHCA to get it fixed quickly with a few other choice words thrown in for impact. Secret Service agents, who are with the president wherever he goes, get, nervous when unexpected and unplanned events unfold.

Political people have short memories when things go wrong. It was a decision they made to let the networks handle the feed during the preliminary discussions so we were out of the loop and they would have to blame someone else, not WHCA. The White House has a lot of power but it doesn't extend to the national news media.

After a long twenty-one minutes, the sound was restored and the debate resumed. I thought the odest thing that occurred was the president and Carter standing on stage, behind their respective podiums, during the twenty-on minutes and totally ignored each other.

Due to all of the traveling during the campaign for president, Marian and the girls stayed in Augusta. Our house was still on the market and we didn't have the financial recourses to own two homes at the same time. One of our detachment commanders owned a townhouse with two bedrooms and said I was welcome to stay with him until our house sold. He was divorced and living by himself. I took him up on his offer. Every time a door is closed to me on this planet, God always opens up another door for me to walk through.

On November 4, 1976, the American people would once again go to the respective voting areas and select the person they felt was best qualified to be president. It was democracy in action, showing how Americans living in a free society can voice their approval or disapproval on who leads our country.

Chapter 22

Jimmy Carter Administration

On November 2, 1976, Governor Jimmy Carter from Georgia was elected to be the 39th President of the United States. It was late evening when the vote count was completed with Carter ending up with 40,826,000 votes and Ford with 39,148,000 votes. The electrical college count was close but not quite as close as the popular vote. The final electrical vote count was 297 for president elect Carter and 240 for President Ford. The most powerful office in the world would once again change hands at noon on January 20, 1977.

After the dust had settled from the exhaustive campaigning, President Ford extended a courtesy to Carter that went beyond the normal presidential transition that takes place when a new president is elected. He signed an executive order directing that telecommunications support would extended to the president elect and his immediate staff.

A team of WHCA personnel were immediately dispatched to establish commutations for the president elect in Plains, Georgia. Actually, incoming carter staff was operating out of the Best Western Motel, in Americus, Georgia. The only buildings in Plains were a few old stores, a couple of churches, and a handful of residential houses including Jimmy Carters. I almost forgot Billy Carters gasoline station.

The next day, I was directed to fly down to Georgia and work with the WHCA team. I guess my boss thought that my being Georgia born may make a difference with the Mr. Carter. It didn't.

The president elect and Mrs. Carter were living in their home in Plains but our first major problem was to find somebody who could set up an appointment so we could brief him on who we were and what sort of communication facilities was installed for him and his staff. The Carter people had made the Best Western their hub for a while so we figured correctly that the motel general manager new who was who and what they did.

We located his personal secretary and she promptly called the governor and set up an early morning appointment the next day. A two position switchboard was installed at the Best Western with direct trunk circuits back to the White House. A secure data facsimile machine and secure teletype was also established.

The Top Secret morning brief that the president receives each morning could now be transmitted to Americus and hand delivered to the incoming president.

The morning brief document is a twenty-four hour summary from the major departments of our government and assembled by the Central Intelligence Agency (CIA). Input is provided by the FBI, State Department, Defense Department, National Security Agency (NSA) and a slew of other agencies.

The next morning, Bob McCormick and I drove to the carter home in Plains and rang the doorbell. After telling Mrs. Carter who we were and why we were there, we were invited in the house and met Governor Carter. He stood up and shook our hands then immediately started back reading the papers in his hands.

Mrs. Carter escorted us throughout the house and suggested places for the phones. We explained to both of them that it was a direct link to our switchboard so all they had to do was pick up the phone and the operators would place their call to whomever they wanted, no matter where they were. These operators were trained to find anyone quickly and they spoiled a lot of presidents with their efficiency. I don't know how they did what they did so quickly but finding people on the telephone was their specialty and they did it well.

At the White House, the Top Secret daily brief is delivered by the National Security Director. For Jimmy Carter, the daily brief would be delivered by a WHCA Warrant Officer. There was no one on site to do the briefing and we certainly didn't have access to its contents. That created some awkward moments at times.

Mr. Carter would open up the pouch and begin reading, then turn and ask a question about its contents. After explaining to him that I did not have access to the documents, he stopped asking, thank goodness.

On January 20, 1977, President Carter was sworn into office at the capitol of the United States. It was freezing cold and I was there. The swearing in ceremony is under the complete control of the

Congressional side of our government and they take pride in making sure everything is done under their control and not the White House.

Consequently, other than making sure the speech is recorded and all Secret Service and White House staff requirements are met, it is uneventful from a technical point of view. From a historical perspective, sometimes I wanted to pinch myself to make sure it was really me who was there.

Each administration that I served under made major changes in how our agency did its job. It took time for the incoming staff to feel comfortable working with our communications personnel, including our commander. They were briefed on the first day in office that our mission was to provide the best communications possible for the Commander-in-Chief of the United States and that we had no political connections or ambitions. Once the staff realized that is how we operated, everyone relaxed and business was back to normal.

After a few months in office, we were notified that the president would be flying to the United Nations to make address the General Assembly. This was not my first trip to New York City but it was to the United Nations (UN) complex. Carter flew by helicopter from Washington, D.C. to a landing pad about six blocks UN. Although the UN is located in the heart of New York City, the land is considered International territory and treated as a sovereign nation. A motorcade was waiting on his arrival to complete the short ride in the presidential limousine.

The Secret Service controls, stores, maintain and fly the car to wherever the president travels. The limousine has extensive armor plating with sophisticated communications gear installed.

There were numerous trips that I made under the carter administration. Not long after his inauguration, trips were scheduled to Caracas Venezuela, Buenos Aires, Argentina, and Tehran Iran. A pre advance team of White House staff, Secret Service, and WHCA Trip Officers departed Andres Air Force early one morning to set up preliminary arrangements for the president trip. I was selected to handle the Caracas Venezuela trip. This would be my second trip to Caracas.

After meeting with the Venezuela government representatives, the advance team departed on their advance preparations mission to other trip locations. I was left to survey the areas the president would be visiting and call back to our operations center and make the necessary request for personnel and equipment. The next morning, I received a telephone call informing me that the trip was cancelled and to fly back to Washington as soon as possible. I probably should have went site seeing but instead, did as I was told and flew back Washington D.C.

My last trip out of country before I retired was a trip to Normandy, France. Normandy beach was where thousands of American soldiers, sailors and marines lost their lives so that we can live in freedom. Adolph Hitler and the German military forces were beginning to lose more battles than they won.

On June 6, 1944, General Dwight Eisenhower, the Supreme European Commander of all forces battling the Nazi regime, launched the battle of all battles to defeat the Germans and Italians and end the war. When visiting Normandy for the first time, it is impossible not to feel the pain, sadness and emptiness suffered by the families of the men who lost their lives during combat.

The name of the person buried is embedded on the white cross lined up in perfect alignment, whether looking North, East, South or West. The national cemetery, which is maintained by the U.S. Government, is located on a cliff overlooking Omaha Beach and the English Channel.

The French had limited telephone capabilities in Normandy. To meet the communications requirement for the White House staff, Secret Service and national news media, we installed a portable microwave link from Bayeux, France to the National Cemetery. Our communications hub was installed at a hotel in Baycux. It was also used by the advance team for hotel accommodations. Overseas trips took longer to coordinate because of having to deal with foreign governments and the ever present language problem. We because well acquainted with the French staff at the hotel during our ten day stay which included Christmas day. This was not the first Christmas I had missed being away from my family and probably wouldn't be my last.

French food is good if you like French food. Bacon and eggs with a side order of grits was not on the menu for breakfast. Neither were hamburgers or hotdogs.

President Carter traveled by train from Paris to Bayeux. On arrival at Bayeux, the presidential limousine was waiting to drive the president to the cemetery which was approximately five miles away.

There were no speeches planned at the cemetery. The entourage who came with him for the trip, walked around in silence while viewing all the graves marked by white crosses. Over 6,000 young Americans made the ultimate sacrifice and their remains are buried there. Although the trip was over thirty years ago, it will always be in my memory.

After a grueling two years, it was now time for me to consider retiring from the Army. I had completed over twenty years of service and my grade was Chief Warrant Officer Four, which at that time, the highest grade for a Warrant Officer. I was already burned out, Marian was tired of living the fact paced lifestyle required in my job and our girls was almost grown. They were basically raised in the Virginia suburbs so now was the time to retire from the Army and move back to Gods country, South Georgia.

In April, 1978, Marian and I drove to Waycross to find a home. After making contact with a local realtor, we decided on a home where I presently live today. The girls were in school so Marian made arrangements for them to stay at home so they wouldn't miss any school days. Our plans were kicking in place for the move but at the last minute, I found out that because of mission requirements, I would not be released until November, 1978.

We had bought the house in Waycross so in June when the school year for Juliann and Elizabeth ended, my family moved back to Waycross. That mean only one thing, I would be living by myself in an apartment for another six months.

Time pasted quickly for me because it was one trip after another. The majority was trips in the United States but there was on to Bonn, Germany. I was hoping I could find some free time to drive up to where we lived for three years but it was impossible. It was just a dream that couldn't be fulfilled.

Chapter 23

Retirement

On November 29, 1978, Marian, Juliann and Beth along with a friend drove up from Waycross to be at my retirement ceremony scheduled for the next day. Although I wore a suit and tie during my ten years of service with The White House Communications Agency, I would be retiring in my military uniform.

The official ceremony took place in the office of our Commanding General located on the 5th floor of the Executive Office Building, next door to the White House. Marian brought my dress uniform and my military ribbons so that I would look like a typical retiring soldier. My uniform still fit except for the headgear. It was too little. I didn't think it could happen to me but I had gotten the Big Head. I felt relieved when Marian spoke up and said no I had not, it was the simple fact my hair was a lot longer now and my head was just a plain old ordinary head Thank goodness.

On the way up in the elevator to the 5th floor, a fellow officer was riding up with us when he glanced over at my uniform and than said, "Tom, you have your ribbons on the wrong side of your uniform. They should be over your heart and not on the right side." When we departed the elevator, he helped place the ribbons correctly so that I would look like a real officer. I don't know why but there is always someone looking out for me.

I was officially a civilian again after twenty-three years of service. A Head of State arrival ceremony was being held on the south lawn of the White House and Marian and the girls wanted to see one last event before we left for Waycross. It would be our last visit inside the security gates of the White House. My diplomatic passport and White House Credentials were stamped "Void," just in case I tried to sneak back in.

Our drive back to Georgia took around twelve hours if we drove without stopping for the night. My car phone had been taken out of the car and my pager which I had to wear at all times, was nowhere to be found. Both were turned in to be used by someone else. I turned to Marian and said, "Nobody knows where I am and nobody cares." She laughed and said, "Isn't that great!" South Georgia, here we come.